The Art of
Catching &
Cooking Crabs

The Shellfish Series is published by Sussex Prints, Inc.,
115 N. Race St., Georgetown, DE 19947

Distributed to the trade by:
Liberty Publishing Company, Inc.
50 Scott Adam Road
Cockeysville, MD 21030

Library of Congress No. 83-61595
ISBN 0-911145-07-9
Second Edition, July 1985
Third Edition, August 1986

Manufactured USA

Table of Contents

Dedication

To my husband Bob, who taught me (almost) everything I know about crabbing.

Acknowledgement

This project would never have been possible without the guidance and help of Robert H. Robinson, author and publisher and my guide in this experience of book writing.

The Art of
Catching & Cooking Crabs

The White House Collection

1

The Crab Persona

The Atlantic blue crab justly deserves its name, for no other creature is as crabby as these hard-shelled denizens of the bays, estuaries and tidal rivers of the east coast.

Feisty, pugnacious, the Atlantic blue crab, "Callinectes Sapidus," has the wherewithal to back up his nasty disposition in two powerful claws which can dispense a great deal of pain when they come in contact with an unwary finger. Respect this fellow.

He may be quarrelsome, but there are times when the blue crab is the epitome of a gentleman. The male crab, called a "Jimmy," is reported to have a courting ritual that would make a peacock blanch with envy. Beginning with an underwater courting dance, the Jimmy attracts his mate and then with a tenderness seldom found in the wild, the courting male crab will cradle and protect the object of his affection for days after their mating.

The reason for this solicitous behavior is because the mating of the Atlantic blue crab is accomplished just after the female or "Sook" has shed her hard shell. The soft-shelled female is defenseless and vulnerable, but the Jimmy will protect her until her shell hardens, in two or three days, by cradling the Sook under his body. Making a guard cage with his legs, the Jimmy will carry the Sook around with him. These odd-looking couples are called "doublers."

Directly translated, Callinectes means "beautiful swimmer" in Greek and the Latin definition of Sapidus is "tasty." Anyone who has sampled blue crabs in any of the many ways they can be served can attest to their tasty reputations, but only those who have ventured down to the shore to observe and catch crabs can know of their admirable ability to get around in their habitat. Blue crabs look awkward and gangling, but can move surprisingly fast, scooting out of sight and out of reach in the blink of an eye when the need arises.

I once observed a blue crab migration of gigantic proportions. They were swimming just below the surface. There were thousands of blue crabs, all about three-inches across the bank, swimming the way crabs do; that is with alternate rapid, sweeping, horizontal strokes across their backs with their two paddle-like swimming legs. Although Atlantic blue crabs have a total of 10 limbs, these are all specialized. The two powerful claws, the largest of their limbs, are for defense and grasping and carrying food to their tiny mouths which are located beneath beady stalked eyes. The six legs are for bottom walking and climbing and the two swimming legs or back fins are for swimming. Crabs can move sideways, forward and backward and hover in the water -- all at slow or very rapid speeds. They also can work their way into the bottom in a flash and remain there with just their stalked eyes protruding, virtually invisible. As John Hay (1838-1905) observed: "There are three species of creatures who, when they seem coming, are going, when they seem going they come: Diplomats, women and crabs."

Photo: Ron Anton Rocz

2

When and Where

The east coast of the United States from Cape Cod, down and around the Florida coast to the Gulf of Mexico, is home for the Atlantic blue crab. These crustacea shun the open waters, preferring the brackish waters of bays, inlets, tidal rivers and the Intracoastal Waterway. When the waters warm up in the spring the recreational crabbing begins as crabs move in from the deep waters into the shallow waters for feeding, molting and reproduction. By spring the water has warmed sufficiently for the weekend crabbers to try their luck and by July the action should be generalized all along the coast. Most will find the early crabs small, except for some notable exceptions which will be discussed in the section on soft-shelled crabs. But as the season progresses, the crabs go through several molts or shedding of their hard shells, increasing approximately one third in size each time. This ecdysis, or molting, is a very critical period in the life of the Atlantic blue crab.

Once its hard shell is shed, and this is done in one piece as the molting crab slowly backs out of its old shell leaving behind what is a whole, but competely hollow crab; the "peeler" or soft-shelled crab results from this process. Prior to its molt, the blue crab has formed another shell underneath its old one. Necessarily so this new shell is soft. Totally vulnerable and totally delectable to many species, not only homo sapiens, soft-shelled crabs will remain that way about three days until their new shells harden.

There is no great secret to finding good crabbing spots. That is, those that are the least bit productive and those that are really hot spots, have in most cases already been tried by someone. Look for telltale signs like old strings tied to pilings of docks and bridges and be on the lookout for commercial crabbers plying their trade, as well as spotting crab pot floats. As already noted, crabs shun open salt water, preferring brackish waters, especially places where a fresh water river, stream or tributary flows. During and after periods of heavy rains the crabs will be found closer to the salt water sources and during periods of little rain or drought, crabs can be found closer to fresh water sources. Also note wind conditions. A day or more of wind blowing from the ocean toward the fresh water source will drive both salt water and the crabs closer to the fresh water source, just as a wind from the fresh water source will push the fresh water and crabs along with it toward the salt water. So, last week's dud crabbing location could be a real hot spot this week if the wind has been blowing the right way. Tides will have a similar effect, but not as drastic, especially the further inland you go.

For soft-shells you will need to walk the eel grass beds to find these in their hiding places. Some are taken in crab pots and traps as "doublers" and others are taken in the spring by "Jimmy potting," which will be discussed in detail later.

Tackle and bait shops are good sources for information on where to crab and what baits are favored locally. As always local knowledge is your most valuable asset.

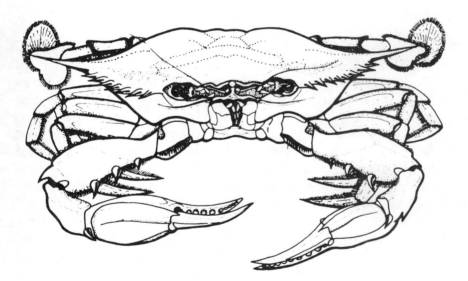

3

To Catch a Crab

Contrary to their reputations of being scavengers of carrion, the Atlantic blue crab does not favor decayed foodstuffs. They aren't too crazy about chicken necks either, but finicky has never been a word applied to blue crabs and they can be caught readily with this bait.

In fact, a chicken neck tied to the end of a line is one of the most popular methods of catching crabs and for the "weekend" watermen," who are often referred to as "chicken neckers," this bait method is one of the easiest to assemble. Other baits, such as a length of eel (traditionally one of the most popular crab baits before eels became known as Oriental and European gourmet delights, most eels now caught are shipped out frozen or live and have become too valuable and too expensive for crab baits) or a fresh fish head (an oily fish is best) can be secured to the end of a length of nylon twine, cotton twine or heavy fishing line. In areas where currents are a problem, line crabbers should use lead weights or sinkers to keep baits on the bottom.

Working from a dock or boat or low bridge, the crabber lowers the bait to the bottom, leaving some slack in the line. After a few minutes' wait the line should straighten out as a feeding crab pulls on the bait. Then it is carefully raised, to reveal a hungry crab clinging to the bait. The crab will let go of the bait when it reaches the surface, so the crabber should have a long-handled crab net (about two-inch mesh) handy to scoop the crab out of the water before this happens.

Empty the crab into a basket or bucket (a dry bucket, not one filled with water since water in a bucket will quickly lose its oxygen and cause the crabs inside it to suffocate) and loosely cover the bucket with wet newspaper or burlap. The hot sun will kill the crabs just as quickly as placing them in a bucket filled with water -- heat, in this case and lack of oxygen, in the other.

One person can man several crab lines and this is one of the best ways to introduce children to the sport of crabbing. There is just enough action to keep them from getting bored and things move slowly enough for them to be in control of the situation.

* * * * * * * * *

Baiting star folding crab trap.

Box folding trap.

Another tending method of crabbing is the star or box folding trap. No dip net is needed for these inexpensive traps. These are baited with a fish head or other suitable bait by securing the bait to the floor of the trap. The traps are used like hand lines, from docks, low bridges or boats in no more than 10 feet of water, any deeper and the crabber would have too much line to handle successfully. Lower the baited trap into the water and its sides will fold out flat once it reaches the bottom. After a few minutes, raise the trap. As it is raised, the sides fold up, trapping the feeding crab inside.

Like line crabbing, several folding traps can be worked by one person at a time, and they all but eliminate the problem of losing the crab at the surface. Folding traps are usually available at tackle shops and hardware stores in areas where crabs can be caught. They are inexpensive and easily transportable.

* * * * * * * * * *

On the St. Johns River in Florida, commercial crabbers used to use a lathe crab pot, but things have certainly changed for the better since those days.

"We used to use those old wooden slat baskets," one commercial crabber recalled. "First you had to put 25 pounds of concrete in it, just to get it to sink and then you'd need a horse to pull it up!"

One of the easiest ways to fill the crab steamer is by using one of the modern crab pots or wire crab traps. These are usually made of plastic coated or galvanized wire that resembles chicken wire. Since an Atlantic blue crab has excellent eye sight, the nearly transparent crab pot is essential and those that are fouled or have marine growth will not catch as many crabs as one the crabs can see through. Some fishermen swear by a sort of a talisman, that is a short length of red ribbon tied so that it hangs inside the crab pot just above the bait basket. Crab pots can be purchased at bait and tackle shops in areas where crabs are caught. Or with a little effort, you can make your own following these instructions:

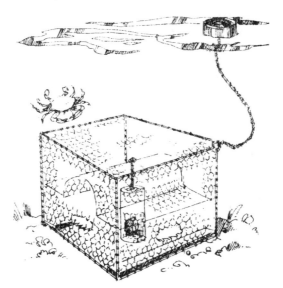

Build Your Own Crab Pot

MATERIALS:

The following is a list of what you will need to build one crab pot. Some materials can be purchased at hardware stores, but you may need to find the crab pot wire at a fisherman's supply house, where you may have to purchase it in a 50- or 100-foot roll or you may be able to convince some commercial fisherman or person who makes crab pots to sell you enough wire for one or two traps.

*15 feet of double-dipped galvanized 1½ inch hexagonal wire mesh, two feet width. (This is special crab pot wire and is not the same as chicken wire. It has been treated to hold up in salt water. Plastic-coated wire is an alternative, although more expensive; it often lasts longer and is easy to work with.)

*1½ feet galvanized ½-inch welded wire. (This is for the bait well and if welded wire is not available, ½- to one-inch hexagonal wire or plastic coated wire can be substituted.)

*20 feet ¼-inch polypropylene or nylon line (more may be needed)

*¼ pound number 4 hog rings

*wire cutters

*needle nose and crimping pliers

*five-inch thin strip of rubber tubing

*six-by-six-inch piece of rubber, aluminum, masonite or thick plastic for bait well door. (A similar size left-over piece of bait well wire can be cut to fit for door.)

*gloves to protect your hands, optional

*several feet of twine

*an empty one-gallon plastic jug or styrofoam float

*One-by-four-inch zinc bar -- can be purchased at net and fishing supply stores, optional.

BEFORE YOU BEGIN:
In these directions, wire will be measured in mesh lengths and widths. Always count the meshes along the selvage, or finished edge.

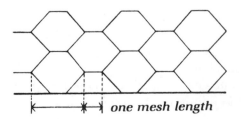

one mesh length

Count one mesh length as the distance from the top point of the hexagon to the bottom point of the hexagon. In between the whole meshes are half meshes. They are not added when counting. For example the wire at bottom left is three mesh lengths, rather than four and a half mesh lengths. It is two mesh widths.

STEP ONE:

Start to work on the floor or other large work space. If working with plastic coated wire, take care not to scuff the coating. Straighten wire flat.

Count two pieces of pot wire 18 mesh lengths and cut, from 15-foot roll. Count five meshes from one end and bend the wire in a 90-degree angle on the next half mesh. To ensure a straight crease, place a two-by-four along the line where the wire is to be bent.

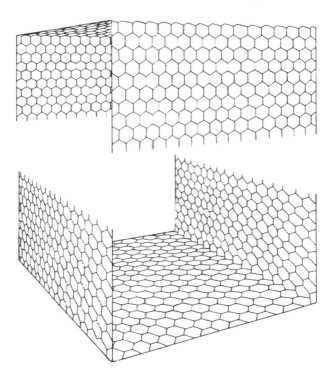

NOTE: Before bending, using a straight measure, measure the next section of eight meshes and be sure this equals the WIDTH of the piece of wire. Since the various types of this pot wire (galvanized and plastic coated) vary according to width and mesh size, it is best to check to see that the two main sections of the trap equal each other before going any further. If they do not equal each other, you will need to adjust your mesh count accordingly.

These show the first bends in making crab trap, using a board as a guide.

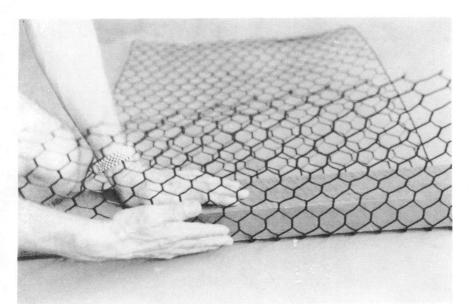

Then count eight meshes and bend the wire again into a 90-degree angle on the next half mesh. You should have five meshes on the third side. The resulting shape should be a square-cornered U. Repeat this procedure with the second piece of wire. Then double-check by fitting the two pieces together so that they form a box. If you've miss-measured, don't panic. The remaining piece of wire should be long enough to cut another side. Use the miss-cut side to cut parlor floor and throats from. This will work if you've cut one of the first two pieces, one or two meshes too short. If one side was cut too long, just trim.

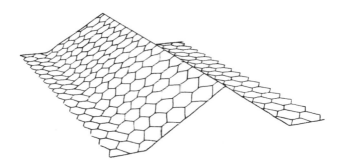

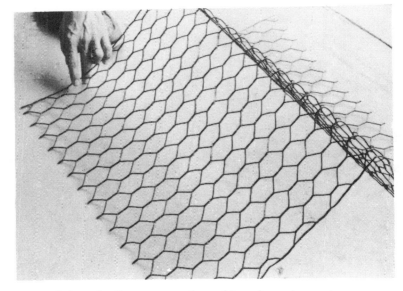

Count two mesh lengths from cut ends and bend, as shown in drawing at top, to form parlor floor.

STEP TWO:

Cut another piece of pot wire 10 mesh lengths. Count five mesh lengths; the next half-mesh should be the center of the wire. In the middle of the half-mesh, bend the wire to an inverted V. Again, a two-by-four may be helpful to get a straight bend.

Working from the cut ends of the V, count two mesh lengths. Bend the wire at the center of the second mesh into a flat position parallel to the floor. This wire will form the floor of the parlor.

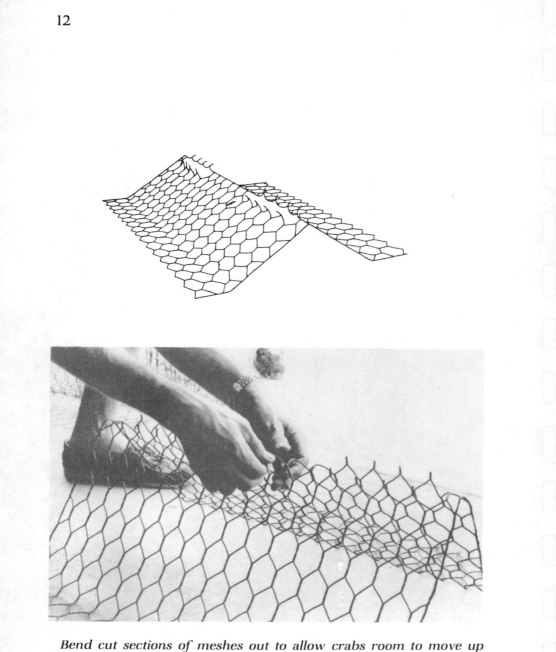

Bend cut sections of meshes out to allow crabs room to move up from bottom chamber to parlor.

STEP THREE:

Next, you will need to cut two holes along the ridge of the inverted V. Count in one half-mesh width on each side and count four meshes. Bend the cut ends upward to form oblong holes at either end of the V. These openings allow the crabs to move from the bottom chamber to the parlor.

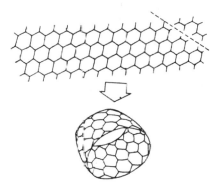

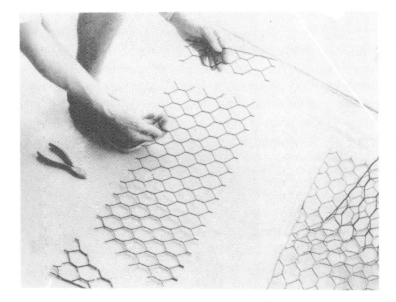

*This shows how to cut entrance funnels. Notice the piece
of pot wire is measured in mesh widths, not lengths.*

STEP FOUR:

To make the throats, or entrance funnels, cut two pieces of pot
wire 13 mesh widths (not lengths) by three mesh lengths. You will
need to trim away some of the width. Cut one mesh off the edge of
the middle row and two meshes off the outside row of each piece, as
illustrated. This will leave you with three rows of 13, 12 and 11 mesh
widths. Bend each piece into a funnel and fasten by twisting cut
ends together.

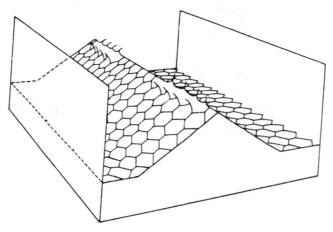

STEP FIVE:

Take one of the pieces you constructed in Step One and place on the floor in a U position. Attach the parlor to the inside of the U, two meshes up from the bottom. The V of the parlor should be inverted.

Fasten with crimping pliers and hog rings or by twisting the cut ends around the top of the second mesh with needle-nose pliers. If hog rings are used, the cut ends must still be bent toward the inside of the pot so you won't be scratched when you're pulling the pot out of the water.

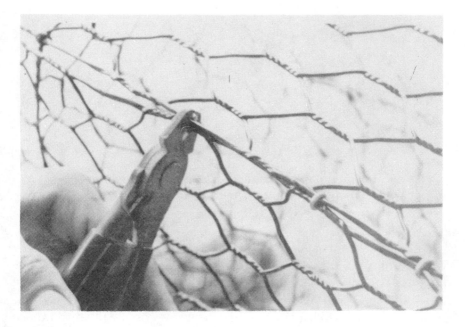

Using hog-nosed pliers

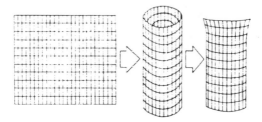

STEP SIX:

To make the bait well, measure the distance from the bottom of the pot to the top of the inverted V. The bait well should be this height and about four inches in diameter. Cut the one-half inch welded wire (or small diameter hexagonal wire) to this size and bend it into a cylinder. Secure the sides and the top with hog rings. If using hexagonal wire, twist cut edges to hold it in the cylinder shape.

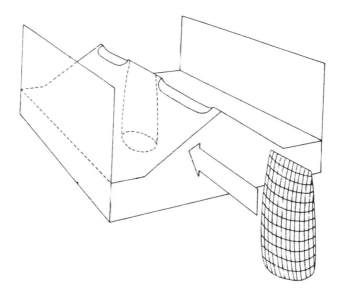

STEP SEVEN:

Place bait well inside trap under the inverted V and, using hog rings, secure it to the bottom of the trap and flattened end at top. Then cut a hole in the bottom of the trap, the diameter of the bait well. Twist cut ends in.

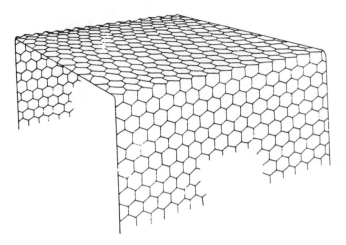

STEP EIGHT:

Take the second piece of wire constructed in Step One and place it in an inverted U position. Along the bottom center of each side cut two holes the same circumference as the large end of the throats, being careful not to cut too large a hole. OR, attach the throats, by twisting the cut ends of wire to the trap sides and THEN cut the holes to insure that they are the correct size. If necessary, trim the length of the throats so that crabs will be able to pass between them and the bait well, easily. If you cut the holes before attaching throats, work from the inside to attach throats and fasten with hog rings or by twisting cut ends.

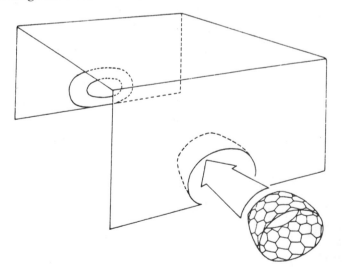

STEP NINE:

Make sure the throats funnel upward and flatten the smaller, or inside end, of the throat slightly into a narrow oblong to accommodate the flat, wide body of the crab.

Some commercial crabbers claim that pots with three or four throats catch more crabs. To build a four-throated pot, simply construct four throats instead of two in step four. After completing step eight, cut two holes along the bottom center of the side of the U-shaped wire piece and attach all throats.

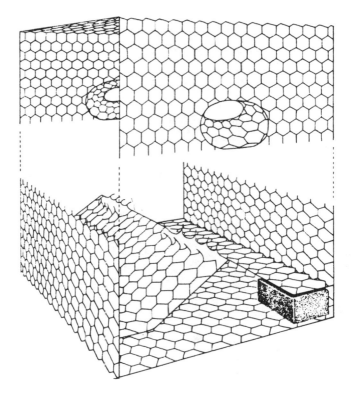

STEP TEN:

Before fastening the pot together, place bricks, rocks or metal bars in two bottom corners of the pot diagonally across from each other. Secure the bricks to the pot with twine or wire. This causes the pot to sink to the bottom. Commercial fishermen often frame their pots with steel reinforcement rods which weight the pots down and make them more durable.

You can wire a zinc bar to the bottom of the pot. Called the sacrificial anode the zinc bar through electrolytic action, slows corrosion of the pot wire caused by salt water. This is not necessary if you use plastic-coated wire.

Place the top of the trap over the bottom and join these pieces with hog rings or by twisting the cut edges around the selvage. Be sure to leave one of the top sides unfastened so the crabs can be shaken from the trap. Secure the selvage edge of the parlor to the side of the pot with hog rings. OR you can make a hinged door to get the crabs out of the pot by cutting some of the leftover wire to form a rectangle about 10 by six inches. Fold cut edges in and secure one side to the top edge of the trap with hog rings (see photo). Then cut an appropriate-size hole and fold cut edges in. Secure with a piece of the rubber strip and hook.

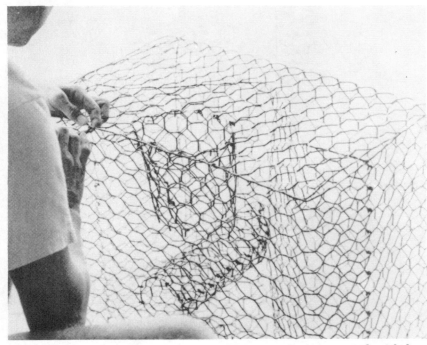

Nearly complete, the trap top and bottom are connected with hog rings and by turning in cut edges of wire.

FINAL TOUCHES:

Attach a six-by-six inch piece of rubber, aluminum, masonite or heavy plastic over the bait well opening. Make a wire hinge on one side of the covering and fasten a hook to the other side so it can be opened when you place the bait in the well.

OR: Using some of the leftover pot wire, cut a square to make a door and fold cut edges in to make a smooth square. Attach one side to the bottom of the trap with hog rings to make hinges. You can attach a strip of the rubber at the unhinged end (see photo) and stretch to slip over trap door when it is to be closed. In this case no hooks are needed, just the strip of rubber, tied at both ends to the trap floor.

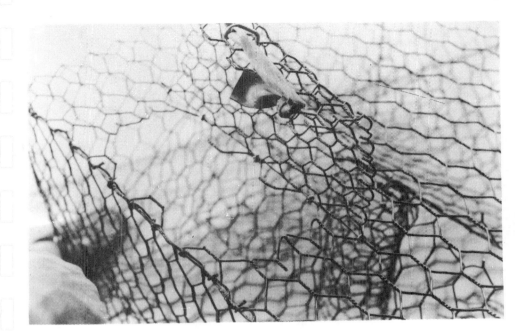

A scrap of pot wire can be cut in a square to make lid for bait well. Just attach a strip of rubber over it and stretch (as shown above) to open lid which uses hog rings to form hinge.

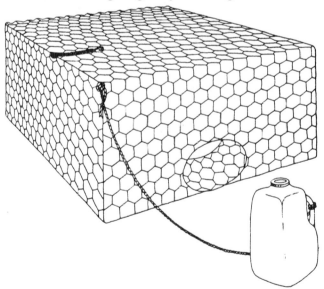

Finally, attach a rope to one of the top corners. Unless you are planning to secure the pot to a dock or pier, tie a buoy to the rope. The buoy can be made from a one-gallon plastic jug and it should be clearly marked.

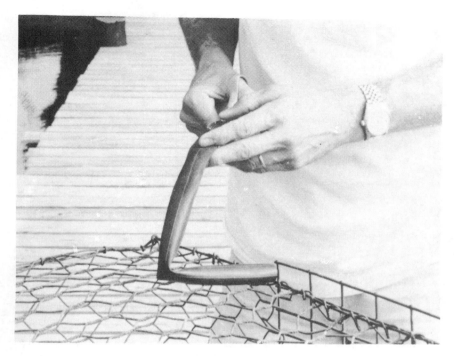

Strips of rubber, like from a bicycle inner tube, are used with wire hooks to close traps. These strips deteriorate and should be replaced when necessary.

HOW THE CRAB POT WORKS:

The crab pot is ready. Fill the bait well with fish heads or other fish remains and secure the cover over it.

Being sure that you have enough line for the pot to rest on the bottom, toss it into the water so that it lands upright. Keep in mind tidal fluctuations. You don't want your pot "high and dry" at low tide and don't want your buoy submerged at high tide. A depth of 10 to 15 feet is a good place to set the pot.

The pot can be left in the water, unattended for several hours. When water temperatures are warm, small fish and minnows will also eat the bait and it will only last about a day. In the winter months the crab bait will last two days or longer.

The blue crab, which is scavenging for its next meal, detects the odor of the bait and will be attracted to the pot. The crab's sensitive antennae search the pot for an opening. Once lured inside the lower

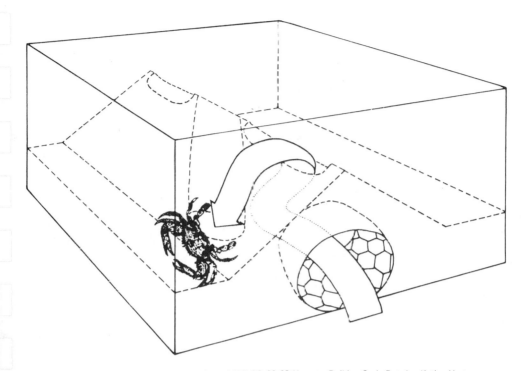

Illustrations of crab pots are from UNC-SG-80-03 How to Build a Crab Pot, by Kathy Hart

chamber of the pot, the crab is thwarted by the bait well. In searching for freedom, the crab swims upward into the trap's parlor. Once inside the parlor, the crab finds escape nearly impossible.

You should check your crab pot at least once a day to remove trapped crabs. Pull the wire apart at the trap opening or, if you have made a trap door, open the door and shake the crabs from the pot into a bucket. You may have to dislodge some of the more stubborn ones with a stick. Remember the crabs will pinch, so do not put your hand in the pot. Crabs should be kept alive in a cool moist place until they are cooked.

< * * * * * * * * *

A boat is not necessary for tending a crab pot, since it can be set alongside a dock or bridge and will produce good results there. But for best catches, you will want to put your trap in about 15 feet of water and a small row or power boat is one good way to put the crab pot out and retrieve it.

Bucket of crab bait -- fish heads.

Mullet heads are one of the favorite crab baits in the Deep South. Crab baits vary according to local availability and generally oily fish are favored for crab baits. In northern regions, herring, killifish or menhaden are popular crab baits. Fish heads are best since they will not fall apart and cannot be torn apart by the feeding crabs so they will remain in your crab pot's bait basket for many hours to attract more crabs.

The best source of crab bait is your local fish market. Take along a bucket and pair of long-handled tongs since you cannot expect the fish monger to supply you with a container for something you will probably be getting for free, or at least at a very low cost. You will probably be directed to an evil-smelling barrel of fish heads and entrails and invited to "help yourself." Using the long-handled tongs, select the freshest-looking fish heads that are just smaller than the diameter of the bait basket on your crab pot. If they are larger you will have to use an axe to chop them down to size.

Another baiting tip: don't use catfish heads for baiting crab pots. While they are perfectly acceptable bait as far as the crabs are concerned, they aren't for the crabber. The head spikes get caught in the cylindrical bait basket and make them nearly impossible -- if not just plain unpleasant when removing the old "ripe" bait to replace it with fresh.

Those who are inveterate fishermen should keep crab bait in mind when cleaning fish and keep a supply of fish heads in the freezer for this purpose. However, in some areas, the use of freshwater game fish or parts thereof for crab bait is unlawful. Check with your local marine patrolman for regulations in your area.

The same goes for crab pot regulations. In some states the legal limit for the non-commercial crabber is five crab pots. And the legal size limit for "keepers" is five inches from point to point across the back of the shell. In nearly all areas it is illegal to keep a "sponge" crab, an egg-carrying female. The spongy-looking egg mass is carried under the female's abdominal apron and by late fall these masses of eggs greatly distend this appendage, making the sponge crabs easy to identify.

Most commercial crab fishermen tend their crab pots, that is haul, remove crabs and replace the bait, each morning, but I believe the evening is the best time to set out or re-bait crab traps since the crabs seem to be more active at night. Freshly-baited traps will attract far more crabs when set out for the night than for the day. If possible, check your traps the following morning. If left in the traps too long, some crabs will eventually find their way out. The smell of the bait will lure crabs to the lower chamber of the crab pot, but they cannot take the bait from the well. Frustrated, the crab will try to escape and its natural tendency will be to swim upward. The crab then goes up into the "parlor" of the trap, where escape is nearly impossible. However, the crab will constantly test its surroundings, sometimes making its way out of the trap or in the case of an old and rusted crab pot, will find a hole to work its way out. Check crab pots frequently for weak spots or holes, especially if you seem to be losing a lot of crabs.

It is reported that a dead crab in a pot will keep others away, so it is doubly important to check traps daily and to change the baits every 24 hours for maximum catches. When there are plenty of crabs moving about, two or three crab pots will yield a bushel of crabs in just a couple days.

Crab pots on land seem to have a penchant for continuing to catch things. The smell of the bait often stays in the traps long after it has been removed. I've heard it will attract cats and on at least one occasion trapped a skunk. The owner of that crab trap hit on a novel plan to remove the potentially odorous visitor. Since skunks are nocturnal animals, they remain pretty docile, sleeping during the day. While I won't claim that removing a sleeping skunk from a crab trap is an easy or carefree matter, it sure beats removing one that is awake and impatient to be about his skunk business. Anyway, that is how that skunk was removed and without incident. Once a hefty

water moccasin found its way inside one of my crab traps which had been left near a dock. I didn't wait to see if it was asleep or awake, but promptly deep-sixed it, that is dumped it in the river.

Just remember when removing crabs from your crab pot, don't reach inside to get them out. They are no friendlier than skunks or snakes. Shake them out or use a stick to dislodge those that cling steadfastly to the mesh.

A 3/8-inch nylon line, 20 to 30 feet long, should be attached to your crab pot and a float attached to the line. Having plenty of line will insure that you won't lose your trap if you should drop it into slightly deeper water. In the tanic-acid stained, brown waters of the St. Johns River, where I set by crab traps, a white styrofoam float two or three feet below the surface would never be seen.

Many commercial crabbers use polypropylene line to attach their floats to their crab pots, but since the line itself floats, they also must weight that line about three feet below the markers. If this is not done, the line floats along the surface and could be cut by a passing motor boat's propeller. To protect your investment in traps, never set them inside channels or where there is heavy boat traffic.

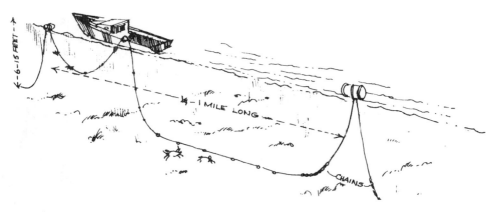

Running the trotline.

Until the advent of light-weight efficient crab traps, trotlines were a popular method of crabbing commercially, especially in the northern regions.

For a trotline you will need a small boat to "run" your crab trotline, along with a prepared line, baits, weights and floats.

To make a crab trotline; attach two short lengths of heavy chain to either end of a 3/8-inch diameter, 100-foot long line. Attach two each of four 20-foot lengths of line to two floats (plastic bleach bottles or styrofoam floats) with a float at each end of the 100-foot line. Secure one of the ends of the 20-foot lines to the chain and the other 20-foot line to an anchor (small boat grapnel or heavy weight). That's your trotline.

To bait the trotline, use salted eel or any tough bait that the crabs can't snatch from the line or eat quickly. Attach the baits at three to four-foot intervals.

Coil the line, with attached baits, and place it in a container with a strong brine solution (four pounds salt to five gallons water). This solution will preserve baits until you are ready to go crabbing. Once the line and baits have been used, they can still be stored, and the baits preserved, in the brine solution until you are ready to go crabbing again.

To lay the trotline, lower one end and then play out the baited line as the boat drifts with the tide or wind. Lower the other end.

Return to the first float and slowly and steadily being pulling the line to the surface, netting the feeding crabs as you come to them.

* * * * * * * * * *

Another method of catching crabs could provide the crabber with enough exercise to acquire a powerful appetite. This requires using

1883 periodical

a dip net and a fleet foot, and it is called "scapping" in some areas, foolish in others. The idea is about as simple as they come. It's that old "man against crab" ploy -- except this one is executed on the crab's turf.

It goes like this: Man takes a long-handled dip net and enters water. Man looks for crab among eel grass, around dock pilings, etc. Hopefully crab does not see man until it is too late and man's dip net has swooped crab from briny deep. Voila!

* * * * * * * * * *

If you don't plan to cook and eat your crabs right away, a holding pen or live box will be necessary. These tough guys, crabs, are in reality fairly fragile creatures which deteriorate quickly after they die. Always discard all dead crabs, whether it's while crabbing or when purchasing live crabs.

The holding pen can be constructed of wire mesh, mesh and wood or entirely of wood slats. A cage of about two by two by three-feet will keep several dozen crabs for about a week. A word of caution though: remember to feed the crabs in the holding box or they will turn cannibalistic. First they will probably eat each others' legs and swim fins and then start killing each other. A few fish heads every other day should satisfy them.

A popular holding pen model on the Chesapeake which my husband used as a child while growing up there was a part wood, part mesh holding box which floated just below the surface. Either a pen that floats just below the surface or one that rests on the bottom would be suitable. But I prefer the one that lowers to the bottom. It not only keeps the crabs where they normally are, it also gives them the opportunity to pick around on the bottom through the bottom of the cage. Don't place your holding pen in an area where the low tide will leave it out of the water or in water so shallow that it will be heated up considerably by the hot sunshine. Locating the holding pen under a dock or in a shaded location is best. Tie it to the dock with a stout line.

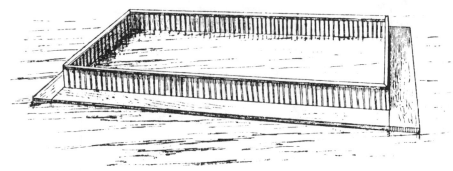

Crab Float or Pound.

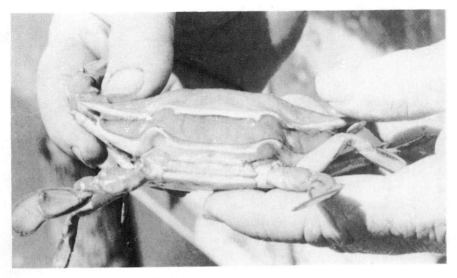

Buster, ready to shed its shell.

The soft-shell is above its smaller old shell.

4

Soft-Shelled Crabs

As popular and widely available as blue crabs and soft-shell crabs have become, there still seems to be some confusion for some about soft-shell crabs. Some are under the misconception that the soft-shell is a different species -- it's not. And then there's this note that appeared in a recently-published cookbook: "Soft-shell crabs have shed the shell and not grown another . . ."

As have been previously mentioned here, the Atlantic blue crab first grows a new shell, a soft one, underneath the hard one -- and THEN sheds the old shell. The new shell is already there, just not hardened yet. This soft shell is edible and so nearly all of a soft-shell crab is eaten when it is prepared.

Crabs periodically shed their shells in order to grow, as all crustacea do. During the Atlantic blue crabs' two to three year life span, they go through at least 21 molts for the males and 18 for the females.

However, for the female crabs, this shedding or "peeling" stage is part of their reproductive cycle. Only soft-shelled Sooks can be impregnated. Before it becomes a sexually mature Sook, the female crab is called a "Sally" or "Snot" in some areas. But with that monumental shed, usually during its second summer of life, the Sally becomes a Sook. The Sook will mate only once in her lifetime.

Commercial crabbers are adept at determining when the Sally or Snot, or the Jimmy, for that matter since he, too, sheds his shell, are about to become "busters" by subtle color variations in their shells and swim fins. Busters are usually set aside to be placed in crab floats or peeling sheds so they can complete the shedding process undisturbed. The result, of course, is the delectible soft-shell crab.

Weak and totally defenseless, the recently-shed Sooks are sometimes found in crab pots, being protected by a galant (but more likely -- a just plain amorous) hard-shelled Jimmy. The two crabs mate at this stage and then the male will continue to cradle the Sook underneath his body in a cage he makes of his legs for the two or three days it takes for the female's new shell to harden. During this time the male uses his strong claws to protect himself and the defenseless Sook.

However, the male soft-shell crab receives no such protection. He must hide from man and fish and others of his own kind as well, who all find the soft-shell a delectible morsel. When the big Jimmys are scarce, the crabbers here say, "Jimmy's out hidin' in the grass, hidin' from the Sook. She'll eat him right up!"

Being somewhat soft hearted, when I come upon one of those shedding crabs in the crab traps I prevail upon my husband to spare the life of this one poor soft shell. After all, who wants to go to the trouble --and frustration -- of preparing and eating just ONE soft-shell crab?

The first one I found in this state was a doubling female which was tenderly put in a tiny-meshed minnow trap since I reasoned that nothing large enough to hurt that crab could enter such a trap.

Anxious to check the progress of the peeling crab, we went out the dock several times that night. The last time we checked we were astonished and dismayed to find a large eel sharing the confinement with a half-eaten soft-shell crab! That eel made fine and "fitting" crab bait and thereafter we plugged the quarter-size entry holes on the ends of the trap whenever we were incubating a soft-shelled crab.

Getting enough soft-shell crabs for a meal is no easy task, but it is not an impossible one. There are several strategies.

In bays and other areas where the water is clear enough to see the bottom, crabbers can wade through the eel grass shallows and literally pick up their dinner of soft-shells where they hide. A glass bottomed bucket is a useful tool for "seeing" the bottom.

As you slowly walk along in the shallow water pay close attention if you should see two crabs together. Crabs are not usually gregarious animals, except when doubling. They are "crabs" in every sense of the word. One of the crabs you see may actually be the recently shed shell with a soft shell resting behind it. The bluish or greenish-looking crab, the larger of the two, is the real one, the soft shell. It won't move as fast as a hard-shell crab and won't pinch as a hard-shelled crab can, but the soft-shell still requires stealth in the approach if the crabber is to be successful.

Late summer is a pleasant time for hunting the soft-shell crab. The crabs are at their biggest then and the water is the warmest and most comfortable for a day's wading. As for exactly when to go soft-shell crabbing, the week before a full moon is most favored. Check the tide also. If it's running in, then choose some other time since crabs usually shed as flood tides begin to ebb. Early in the day is the best time if all other conditions are right. But night hunting with a light is also successful in many areas and is a popular way to collect soft-shell crabs in the South. The grass beds again are the place to look at night, with a strong battery-powered lantern illuminating the bottom.

Not all female crabs become sexually mature Sooks during their second summer and because of this situation, crabbers have learned to take advantage of this quirk in the crab's system of things by "Jimmy potting."

Each spring there is a proportion of the crab population, third summer females, which did not shed in time in the previous fall to become impregnated. These big Sallys are ready and anxious to mate -- out looking for the Jimmys.

Crabbers in the know usually are out Jimmy potting in the latter part of May. They place one or two Jimmys in an unbaited crab pot and wait for the impassioned females to take this bait. One Jimmy can attract several females before he supposedly gets tired of the scam. The females are -- of course -- busters at this stage, ready to shed their shells and, if kept for a day or two, will become soft-shell crabs. It should be mentioned that there is a very high mortality rate among peelers, from predators of course, but also from natural causes since the process of ecdysis is a perilous one for the crab. Some simply don't survive the process.

Carefully place soft-shell crabs on and under a light bed of wet seaweed or wet burlap and out of the sun. They can be kept this way for several hours while you are catching enough for dinner. Sprinkling them with some crushed ice is also a good idea to keep them alive and fresh. Once home, keep the soft-shell crabs in the refrigerator until ready to clean and prepare them. Uncooked soft-shell crabs can be kept in a refrigerator several days.

Parts of a Crab

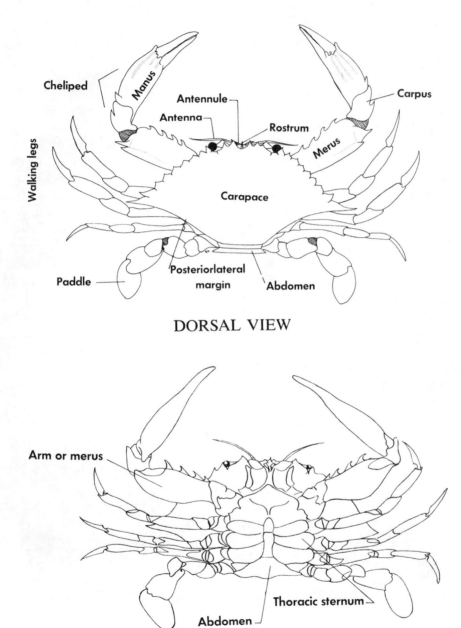

Cheliped

Manus

Antennule

Antenna

Rostrum

Carpus

Merus

Walking legs

Carapace

Paddle

Posteriorlateral
margin

Abdomen

DORSAL VIEW

Arm or merus

Thoracic sternum

Abdomen

VENTRAL VIEW

5

From the Pots to the Pot

One of the most useful tools you will find for crabbing -- aside from your traps and cooking pot -- will be a large pair of long-handled tongs.

A pinch from a blue crab is no laughing matter. Blood poisoning has been known to result. So use tongs whenever handling crabs.

Also, contamination of cooked crabs should be avoided by never letting cooked crabs come in contact with uncooked crabs, or even with buckets or utensils or other containers which have held uncooked crabs.

Discard any dead crabs before cooking and if you are buying live crabs, buy only the frisky ones. Refuse limp, lifeless crabs. If any die before they reach the cooking pot, discard them quickly since bacteria multiplies rapidly and may kill others in your container.

On the other hand, once healthy crabs have been cooked, they can be kept refrigerated about two days or frozen for up to two months. Cooked crabs (see general cooking instructions in following section) can be cleaned, picked and the meat packed into containers, with no water or other liquid added, sealed and frozen at 0 degrees F for up to two months.

One ardent crabber I have heard of, swears by freezing crab meat in a cushion of skim milk to keep it from becoming stringy when defrosted. If this is a problem you have experienced, you might want to try this method. And what do you do with the milk once the crab is defrosted? Well, you could offer it to the cat.

A former neighbor of mine who was concerned about steaming squirming crabs (she said she couldn't stand the sounds of them scratching inside the pot) would slip them inside the freezer for a few minutes to calm them down. Sometimes she would just leave them in the freezer when she didn't have time to cook and clean them and would cook them at a later date. She claimed that freezing the uncleaned, live crabs did not effect their taste or texture. Just remember that cold, unlike heat, does not kill bacteria and those frozen crabs are just as susceptible to contamination as fresh ones. Keeping this in mind, you can experiment and find the method which works best for you.

Picking the meat from cooked crabs is not the head-scratching, puzzling enigma it may at first seem. Divide and conquer is the key here.

Granted, cleaning whole cooked crabs is somewhat messy, but the comraderie established over a Saturday night crab boil is more than worth the mess involved. Besides they are delicious.

Crab pickers seem to be of two philosophies: There are those who pick and eat . . . pick and eat . . . pick and eat. And then there are those who pick and pick and pick and pick and THEN eat and eat and eat. There is no use trying to convert one religion to another, just be sure to have plenty of cold beer and rolls of paper towels handy.

Regular Crab Knife

Professional Crab Knife

1. The secret to successful picking lies in the use of the crab knife. While special knives are available, any small, heavy knife can be used.

Cleaning a Cooked Hard Shell

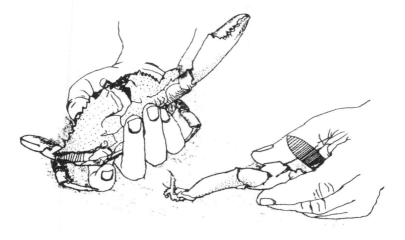

2. Remove the claws by pulling them away from the body. Save any meat attached to the end of the "arm".

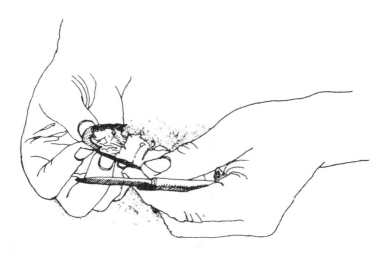

3. Holding the crab knife near the end of the handle, crack the claws and remove the meat. If the meat does not come out easily, pry it out of the shell with the knife.

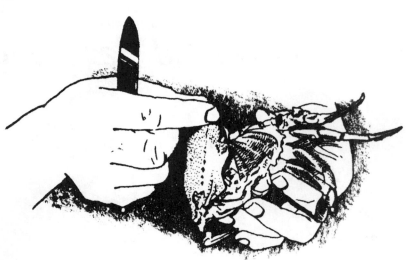

4. *Grasp the shell near one of the spines and pull up on it, removing the back. Discard the back, which has no meat in it.*

5. *Once the back has been removed, the fat and the gills are clearly visible.*

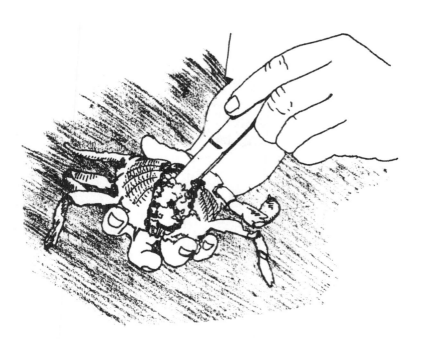

6. Using the knife, scrap away the yellowish material, called the fat, lying in the middle of the crab. Some people relish the fat, but most find it rather strong tasting.

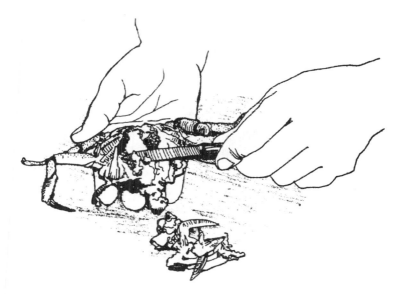

7. Once the fat has been removed, the next step is to cut away the gills, which are the gray feathery structures found on either side. The gills are called the "dead man" in the low country and should not be eaten.

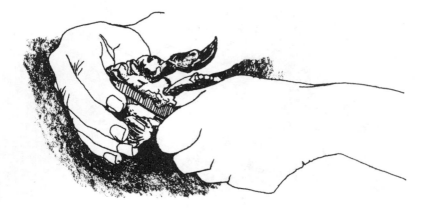

8. *Cut away the walking legs and remove any bits of meat clinging to the cut ends.*

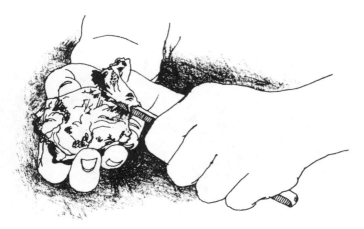

9. *Slice off the top right side of the body and set it aside. Do the same to the left side.*

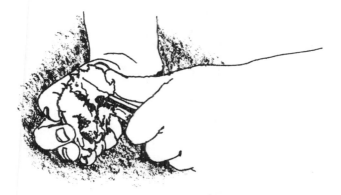

10. With the point of the knife remove the lump meat from the rear portion of the body. Now remove the meat from the remaining sections by prying upward with the knife.

11. Take one of the sides removed earlier and pick out the meat. Do the same to the other side.

Illustrations of opening crabs are from Dipping & Picking, published by the Sea Grant Advisory Program, South Carolina

Cleaning Uncooked Crabs

A second option on crab picking is to clean the crabs before they are steamed. This involves a quick and humane death. A St. Johns River crabber showed me how, but the practice is pretty widespread. The method is mentioned in a 19th Century British work describing the lives of the laborers and poor there. "I kill my crabs before I bile them. I stick them in the throat with a knife and they're dead in an instant. Some sticks them with a skewer, but they kick a good while with the skewer in them. It's a shame to torture anything when it can be helped," explains a street seller of shellfish in the old book.

The process I learned is much the same as the book describes, but it is the crab's brain which is pierced causing almost instant death. The apron and back shell are then pulled away and the intestines and lungs are scraped out with a knife. The crabber who showed me how to kill and clean crabs before cooking, however, did not scrape out the insides of the crabs. Instead, he broke the crabs in two at the midsection indention after the back shell was removed. Then, holding the half tightly in one hand, he deftly slung the soft matter out of the crab in one swift motion, splattering the side of a nearby shed. Needless to say, this method is best practiced a good distance from the house.

Crabs cleaned before cooking should only be steamed since they may absorb too much water if boiled. Also in this case, add the spices to the steaming liquids rather than sprinkling them on the crabs, as is usually done with steamed crabs. The meat of pre-cleaned crabs is exposed and will absorb just the right touch of the spices from the steam, but would be inedible if the strong spices were coating it.

1. *Using long-handled tongs, turn a frisky live crab upside down. At the indicated point, plunge ice pick deep into shell and rotate in a small circle until crab relaxes. This should occur within seconds after the shell is penetrated. The crab is dead.*

2. *Grasping apron on abdomen, peel back and pull back shell away. Either discard this shell or clean thoroughly and boil or bake shell for use as a "baking shell" for various crab dishes.*

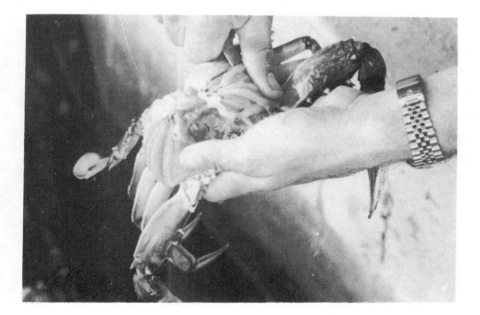

3. *Scrap away lungs and innards. If desired - crabs can be broken in half along the midsection indention and each half slung briskly to remove intestines. Avoid excessive washing after shell has been removed since meat will absorb too much water. But a light quick rinse will effectively remove what is left of soft material.*

Cleaning Soft-Shelled Crabs

Since the shell of a soft-shell crab is eaten with the rest of the crab, these tasty morsels are simple to clean.

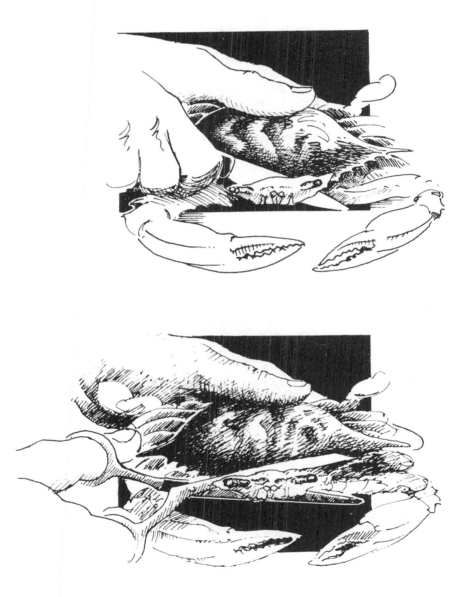

1. Holding the soft-shell in the palm, cut the face from the crab with kitchen sheers or place crab on board and use a sharp knife to cut.

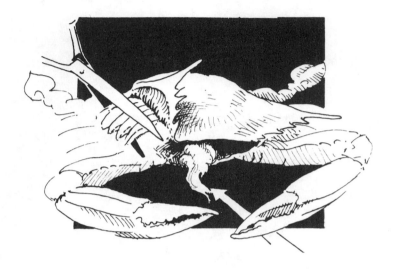

2. Lift shell points and cut away gills or lungs.

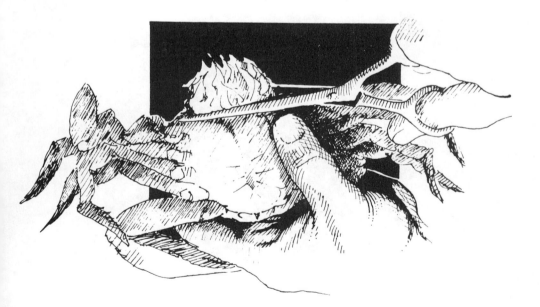

3. Cut away apron, underside of crab. Rinse gently with water and drain well. Cook or freeze.

To freeze soft shell crabs, wrap the cleaned crabs in a double layer of waxed paper or single layer of freezer paper and seal in plastic freezer bags or containers. Soft-shells prepared this way can be safely frozen at 0 degrees F for up to two months.

Canning Crab Meat

Another method of preserving crab meat for use later is to can the cooked meat.

NOTE: Home canned shellfish is highly susceptible to botulism contamination. Only a pressure canner may be used for processing and scrupulous care and attention to recipe details is essential for success. Use only new jars made for pressure canning and new two-piece screwband lids. For further information on home canning of crabs, write to the U.S. Department of the Interior Fish and Wildlife Service and request Conservation Bulletin No. 28, Home Canning of Fishery Products.

While freezing is preferable, brining and canning is a good method of preserving large quantities of crabs when other methods are not available.

For one dozen half-pint jars, you will need 25 pounds of live crabs. Kill and clean crabs before cooking (see previous section for illustrations and instructions). Using one cup pure pickling salt and one-quarter cup lemon juice to each gallon of water, use enough water that will cover crabs and bring water to a boil. Dump in crabs and bring to a boil again. Boil 15 minutes. Remove crabs and cool. Pick out meat, separating claw and leg meat from the back meat. Wash meat with a gentle spray of water to get rid of curds of coagulated protein. Press excess moisture from meat.

Have ready an acid blanch (to eliminate harmless darkening of crab meat during processing) of one cup salt, one gallon water and one cup lemon juice for each 15 pounds of crab meat. With a colander or metal (but not aluminum) basket, dip crab meat (claw for two minutes and body meat for one minute) into solution. Press out excess moisture and drain meat well.

Pack clean jars with crab meat, leaving one-half inch head room.

Half close jars and "exhaust" at zero pounds until inside of jars is 170 F. This takes about 10 minutes. Screw bands tightly and pressure process at 10 pounds (240 F) for 65 minutes. Remove from hot water and air cool.

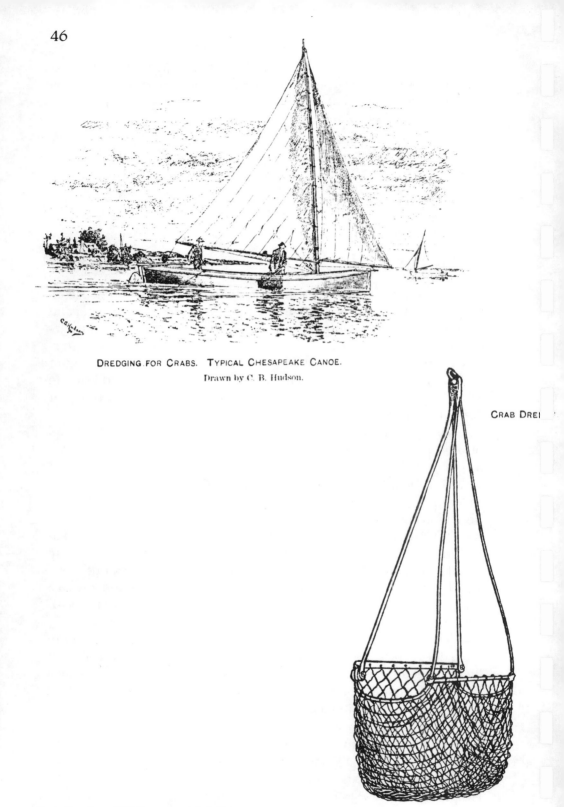

DREDGING FOR CRABS.   TYPICAL CHESAPEAKE CANOE.
Drawn by C. B. Hudson.

CRAB DRE

Illustrations from 1889 Government Bulletine

6

Let's Eat

A good source of protein, the Atlantic blue crab also contains some minerals and vitamins. If cooked by the steaming method, the meat will also offer Vitamin A. There are about 90 calories in each one half cup of picked meat, while the average soft-shell contains 185 calories. Atlantic blue crab is not only flavorful, but is versatile too and is available in a variety of forms.

Crabs can be caught or purchased live or cooked in many areas where they are caught. Commercially frozen, pasteurized and canned blue crab meat is widely available -- as are frozen pre-prepared crab meat dishes. Canned crab meat is available in lump, flake, lump and flake, and claw. This form of crab meat requires no refrigeration and has a long shelf life, making it a convenient choice for various dishes. The lump, being solid choice white meat, is more costly than the flake or claw meat. Choose lump meat when appearance counts, as in seafood cocktails and cold salads. Flake canned crab meat is good for use in dips, spreads and casseroles. The brownish claw meat is not as attractive but is every bit as flavorful, as the others. It is a good choice for crab cakes and is lower in price than lump or flake styles. Drain and rinse canned crab meat. Pick over the meat to remove bits of shell or cartilage.

* * * * * * * * * *

Fresh blue crabs should be kept alive until the time they are steamed or boiled, the exception being the previously described method of killing and cleaning of crabs immediately before cooking.

Boil or steam? The preference is purely personal and sometimes regional. While steamed spiced crabs are the traditional fare of the Chesapeake Bay region, in the Deep South blue crabs are more often boiled. Sometimes with the addition of potatoes, corn, shrimp and even eggs in the shell, this typical Southern-style boiled seafood dinner brings to mind a New England clam bake in which a whole meal is steamed together.

Whatever way you choose to prepare your crabs, you are in for some good eating. Using either the boiled or steamed methods, your cooked crabs can be eaten as is, accompanied by pitchers of frosty beer. Or pick the meat from the cooked crabs to prepare in any of the recipes that follow, or pick, pack and freeze the meat for later use. For some of the following dishes, you and your family and guests will want to roll up your sleeves to tackle the Atlantic blue crab, while for others you will want to make sure the table is set with your best china and that the wine is chilled to perfection since you will have entered the realm of gourmet cooking. You have found that the Atlantic blue crab is good sport, but now you will see that this crusty little fellow is indeed not only tasty, but versatile too.

Boiled Crabs

Live Atlantic blue crabs, about 12 per person
Boiling water
½ cup salt
3 tablespoons commercial crab boil spices
1 cup vinegar

Fill a large pot, an enamel canning pot is suitable, two thirds full of water. Add salt and bring to a boil. Add vinegar, spices and crabs and continue to boil 15-20 minutes, or until crabs turn bright red and are cooked. Remove crabs to cool.

NOTE: Boiled crabs are traditionally eaten at a newspaper-covered table. Wooden mallets, nut crackers or even short lengths of wood are provided to diners to crack open claws. Special solid-handled crab knives are available which can be used to strike crab claws to crack them and also to remove meat from body cavities. It is a messy meal and diners also will need plenty of paper napkins or paper toweling and cold libations. Beer is traditionally served to accompany the spicy meal.

Steamed Crabs

Live Atlantic blue crabs, about 12 per person
2-3 tablespoons commercial crab seasoning, available in most groceries and seafood markets
3 tablespoons salt
Water and vinegar

Using a large pot, an enamel canning pot is suitable, you will need a rack to keep the crabs off the bottom of the pot. A simple rack can be constructed of clear pine (see photograph) and reused each time you steam crabs. Wire racks are not suitable since they rust with the large amount of salt and corrosive spices and vinegar used in the steaming process.

Using equal amounts of water and vinegar, add enough to cover bottom of pot about three inches deep. Place live crabs on top of rack and sprinkle with salt and spices. Cover and, over high heat, bring liquid to a boil and steam crabs about 20 minutes, or until they turn red.

A wooden rack like this is needed to steam crabs. This rack is simple to make and can be reused whenever crabs are steamed. Measure bottom of pot in which crabs will be steamed. Cut one-by-one-inch lengths of pine, or other suitable wood which will not impart its flavor to the food, to fit the bottom. Nail together to form rack and using a rasp or saw, round outside edges so rack will fit inside pot. To season the rack, boil it with salt and vinegar in water for five minutes before it is used the first time. After use, do not use soap to clean rack. Simply scrub and rinse with fresh water, since soap may be absorbed by the wood and it will give the next batch of crabs an "off" or perfume-y flavor. The rack may need to be stored outside, for no matter how much rinsing and scrubbing it gets, it will still retain the crab odor. Hang it where animals cannot get to it.

Appetizers

Crab meat shows its versatality in dazzling arrays of appetizers and hors d'oeuvres and one of the most popular uses of crab for pre-dinner nibblers is in crab dips. The adaptations are endless, but here are some of the best:

Crab Dip I

1 cup crab meat or one seven and one-half ounce can crab meat, drained, rinsed and picked over to remove shell and cartilage
1 cup mayonnaise
½ cup dairy sour cream
1 teaspoon lemon juice
3 teaspoons dry sherry
Freshly ground pepper and salt to taste

Combine all ingredients, blending well. Refrigerate until ready to serve. Serve chilled with chips or crackers. Makes two cups.

Crab Dip II

1 cup crab meat
⅓ cup heavy cream
2 teaspoons lemon juice
1 teaspoon Worcestershire sauce
Dash garlic powder
1 eight-ounce package cream cheese
Salt and pepper to taste

In blender or food processor, place heavy cream, lemon juice, cream cheese, Worcestershire sauce and garlic powder. Whirl or process until smooth, about 10 seconds.
Add crab meat and whirl to mix in. Season to taste with salt and pepper. Makes one and three quarters cups. Chill and serve cold with chips or crackers.

Crab Dip III

1 cup dairy sour cream
1 envelope dry Italian salad dressing mix

1 cup crab meat or one seven and one-half ounce can crab meat

Combine all ingredients and serve chilled with chips or crackers. Makes about two cups dip.

Crab Dip IV

1 cup crab meat
Juice of one lemon and two dashes hot pepper sauce
1 teaspoon Worcestershire
1 eight-ounce package cream cheese
½ cup sour cream
½ cup mayonaise
2 tablespoons minced green onions, including green tops
1 clove garlic, minced
1 teaspoon grated horseradish

Combine crab meat with lemon juice, hot pepper sauce and Worcestershire. Set aside and beat cream cheese and sour cream. Beat in mayonnaise and onion and garlic. Stir in horseradish and fold in crab meat. Serve chilled with potato chips or crackers. Makes about two and one-half cups dip.

Crab Dip V

1 cup crab meat or one seven and one-half ounce can crab meat
1 cup smooth cottage cheese
2 teaspoons dill seed
1 teaspoon Worcestershire sauce
2 tablespoons buttermilk
1 tablespoon lemon juice
½ teaspoon salt
Freshly ground pepper to taste
¼ cup chopped, seeded cucumber

Combine all ingredients and add more buttermilk if necessary to obtain a good consistency. Makes about two and a quarter cups dip. Serve chilled with chips or crackers.

Pink Crab Dip

1 cup crab meat or one seven and one-half ounce can crab meat
2 tablespoons sour cream
3 tablespoons ketchup
2 tablespoons minced onion
1 eight-ounce package cream cheese, creamed
1 teaspoon Worcestershire sauce

Combine all ingredients and serve chilled on crackers or with vegetables to dip. Makes about two and a half cups dip.

Crab and Shrimp Dip

2 cups crab meat or two seven and one-half ounce cans crab meat
1 pound cooked shrimp, cooled and shelled
1 three and one-half ounce can mushrooms
1 cup chopped green onions, tops included
1 cup butter
1 cup all-purpose flour
1 six-ounce can evaporated milk, undiluted
2 cups milk
1 cup fresh parsley
1 teaspoon paprika
½ teaspoon pepper
Salt to taste

Cut shrimp in small pieces and combine with crab meat. Melt butter in a two-quart saucepan. Saute' onions until soft and saute' mushrooms briefly. Stir in flour until smooth and cook until thickened slightly. Slowly stir in evaporated milk and milk, stirring constantly. Cook until smooth and thickened. Add shrimp and crab and seasonings. Serve hot with corn chips. Makes about one quart dip.

Hot Crab-Cheese Dip

1 cup crab meat or one seven and one-half ounce can crab meat
½ pound sharp process cheese, cubed
10 ounces sharp Cheddar cheese, cubed
½ cup milk
½ cup dry white wine

Drain, rinse and pick crab meat, if using canned. Set aside. Combine cheeses with milk in heavy saucepan or fondue pot. Stir over low heat until the cheese melts. Stir in wine and crab meat. Heat through. Serve hot with crackers or chunks of bread. Makes about three cups dip.

Crab spreads come next and whether you choose hot or cold spreads, they are one special way to dress up party breads or crackers.

Hot Crab Spread

2 cups crab meat or two seven and one-half ounce cans crab meat
½ cup mayonnaise
1 cup green onions, tops included, chopped
2 eight-ounce packages cream cheese, softened
⅓ teaspoon hot red pepper sauce
1 teaspoon Worcestershire sauce
Slivered almonds - about two tablespoons

Combine all ingredients and spread in a casserole. Top with almonds. Bake at 350 degrees for 20 minutes and serve hot with crackers.

Crab Spread

1 seven and one- half ounce can crab meat
½ cup mayonnaise
1 tablespoon minced chives or green onion tops

Juice of one half of a lime
1 tablespoon sherry
½ tablespoon tarragon
¼ teaspoon salt
Dash red pepper

Place all ingredients in food processor or blender and whirl briefly to combine. Serve on bread or crackers. Makes about one and a quarter cups spread.

Crab Ball

1 cup crab meat
1 eight-ounce package cream cheese
Worcestershire sauce to taste
1 teaspoon lemon juice
2 drops hot pepper sauce

Soften cream cheese and combine with other ingredients. Roll into a ball shape and refrigerate overnight. Make a sauce of:

½ cup chili sauce
Horseradish and lemon juice to taste

Combine and drizzle over crab balls before serving with crackers or assorted party breads.

Party Crab Balls

1 cup crab meat
¼ cup minced onion
1 cup cracker meal
2 tablespoons chopped parsley
½ cup condensed beef consomme'
1 egg, beaten
1 tablespoon mustard
1 teaspoon Worcestershire
¼ cup mayonnaise
Cornflake crumbs

Combine all ingredients, except for cornflake crumbs. Chill at least one hour. Form into about 40 one-inch balls and roll in cornflake crumbs.
Place on a baking sheet and bake at 375 degrees for six minutes.

Crab balls may be frozen after rolling in cornflake crumbs for future use. If frozen, bake 10 minutes.

Serve hot with toothpicks and a sweet and sour sauce for dipping. Makes about 40.

Crab-Bacon Rolls

12 slices bacon
½ cup tomato juice
1 egg, beaten
1 cup breadcrumbs
½ teaspoon salt
¼ teaspoon pepper
1 teaspoon Worcestershire
1 tablespoon chopped parsley
1 cup crab meat or one seven and one-half ounce can crab meat

Cut bacon slices in half and set aside. Combine remaining ingredients and divide into 24 portions. Shape into little rolls and wrap each with a piece of the bacon and fasten with a pick.

Broil (550 degrees) 10 to 12 minutes, turning often to cook evenly. Drain on paper toweling and serve hot. Makes two dozen.

Crab Fingers

One of the easiest (and best) ways to serve crab in appetizer form is "crab fingers" which are nothing more than the steamed or boiled crab claws which have been chilled and pre-cracked so the diners can just slip the morsel of meat out and dip it in spicy-hot cocktail sauce spiked with horseradish. Count on about a dozen "crab fingers" for each person served.

Crab-Mushroom Canapes I

1 cup crab meat
⅔ cup undiluted cream of mushroom soup
1 tablespoon minced green pepper
1 tablespoon chopped pimiento
1 tablespoon sherry
Salt and pepper to taste
Toasted bread rounds
Buttered bread crumbs

Combine crab, soup, pepper, pimiento, sherry, salt and pepper and heat through.

Spread bread rounds with crab mixture. Sprinkle with bread crumbs and brown lightly under broiler. Serve hot.

Crab-Mushroom Canapes II

2 cups crab meat
1 cup cooked sliced mushrooms
4 tablespoons heavy cream
5 drops hot pepper sauce
Salt and pepper to taste
Bread rounds, toasted on one side
Anchovy butter
¼ cup each grated Parmesan cheese and buttered bread crumbs

Combine crab meat, mushrooms, cream, salt, hot pepper sauce and pepper. Spread untoasted sides of bread rounds with anchovy butter and then spread with crab meat mixture. Sprinkle with cheese and buttered bread crumbs.

Bake at 425 degrees for eight to 10 minutes or until lightly browned.

Crab-Swiss Bites

1 cup crab meat or one seven and one-half ounce can crab meat
1 cup shredded Swiss cheese
1 tablespoon minced green onion
½ cup mayonnaise
1 teaspoon lemon juice
¼ teaspoon curry powder
1 package refrigerated flaky-style rolls (12)
1 can (five ounces) water chestnuts

Mix crab meat with grated cheese, onion, mayonnaise, lemon juice and curry powder. Separate each roll into three layers and place on an ungreased baking sheet. Spread crab mixture on each and top with thin slices of water chestnuts. Bake at 400 degrees, 10 to 12 minutes, or until golden brown. Makes 36.

Crab-stuffed Mushrooms

12-18 medium fresh mushrooms
1 cup crab meat
2 tablespoons salad oil
1 egg, beaten
2 tablespoons mayonnaise
2 tablespoons minced onion
1 teaspoon lemon juice
2 tablespoons melted butter
Soft bread crumbs, about one-half cup

Rinse mushrooms and pat dry. Remove stems and brush caps with salad oil and arrange on an oiled baking sheet.

Combine crab, egg, mayonnaise, onion, lemon juice and one-quarter cup bread crumbs. Stuff caps with this mixture.

Mix one-quarter cup bread crumbs with melted butter and sprinkle over stuffed mushrooms. Bake at 375 degrees for 15 minutes. Makes 12 to 18.

Deviled Crab Canapes

1 cup crab meat
1 tablespoon butter
1 tablespoon onion juice
1 teaspoon Worcestershire
½ teaspoon prepared mustard
¼ cup thick white sauce

Combine all ingredients and heat through. Serve hot on crackers or toasted bread rounds.

Crab-stuffed Tomatoes

1 pint cherry tomatoes (25-30)
1 cup crab meat
2 tablespoons chopped green onion
1 teaspoon lemon juice
¼ cup mayonnaise
Salt and pepper to taste
A few drops hot pepper sauce

Hollow tomatoes and invert and drain. Mix remaining ingredients and stuff tomatoes. Serve chilled on a bed of ice garnished with parsley or chopped lettuce.

Crab-stuffed Eggs

12 hard cooked eggs
1 cup crab meat
½ cup chopped almonds
½ cup minced celery
2 tablespoons minced green pepper
1 teaspoon prepared mustard
Salt and pepper to taste
Mayonnaise to moisten

Slice eggs in half and remove yolks. Mash yolks and combine with remaining ingredients. Stuff whites and serve chilled. Makes 24 deviled eggs.

Crab-stuffed Artichokes

6 artichoke bottoms
1 cup crabmeat
Mayonnaise to moisten

Combine crab meat with enough mayonnaise (about one to two tablespoons) to moisten. Mound on artichoke bottoms. Serves six.

Salads

Crab-Avocado Cocktail

1½ cups crab meat, preferably lump
1 large ripe avocado, peeled, pitted and cubed
¾ cup diced celery
½ cup mayonnaise
1 tablespoon lemon juice
Salt and pepper to taste
Heavy cream to moisten
Lettuce leaves

Toss crab, avocado and celery with a mixture of the mayonnaise, lemon juice and enough cream to make sauce of coating consistency. Season with salt and pepper. Serve well chilled on lettuce leaves. Serves four.

Hot Crab Salad I

2 cups crab meat
1 cup thinly sliced celery
½ teaspoon salt
1 small onion, minced
½ cup unsalted cashew nuts
1 cup mayonnaise
2 tablespoons lemon juice
1 cup crushed potato chips
½ cup shredded Cheddar cheese

Combine all ingredients, except for potato chips and cheese. Pile in casserole or individual baking dishes. Sprinkle with the cheese and potato chip crumbs and bake at 400 degrees about 20 minutes, until mixture is heated through and cheese is melted. Serves six.

Hot Crab Salad II

1 seven and one-half ounce can crab meat
½ cup chopped green pepper
½ cup diced celery
¼ cup toasted, shredded almonds
1 small onion, chopped
½ cup mayonnaise
½ teaspoon Worcestershire
Salt and pepper to taste
Buttered bread crumbs, about one-half cup

Combine all ingredients, except for bread crumbs. Pile in casserole or two individual baking dishes and top with bread crumbs. Bake at 350 degrees for about 30 minutes. Serve hot. Serves two.

Chinatown Crab Salad

2 cups lump crab meat
1 can water chestnuts, chopped
¾ cup chopped celery
½ cup toasted slivered almonds
2 tablespoons minced onion
½ cup sour cream
½ cup mayonnaise
Salt and pepper to taste
1 can (three ounces) Chinese noodles
Lettuce leaves

Combine all ingredients, except for Chinese noodles and lettuce leaves. Immediately before serving, toss in noodles and serve on beds of lettuce. Or, serve garnished with Chinese noodles. Serves six.

Crab Louis

¼ cup chili sauce
2 tablespoons minced fresh parsley
2 teaspoons vinegar
¾ cup homemade mayonnaise
½ teaspoon Worcestershire
¼ teaspoon grated horseradish
1 pound lump crab meat
Lettuce leaves

Combine the first six ingredients and chill. Serve in lettuce cups. Serves four.

Luncheon Crab Salad

1 cup crab meat
½ cup sliced celery
1 tablespoon sliced green onion, including tops
2 tablespoons sliced, pitted ripe olives
½ cup mayonnaise
3 hard-boiled eggs, sliced
1 medium cantaloupe, chilled

Combine first four ingredients and season with salt and pepper. Fold in mayonnaise and two of the sliced eggs. Chill while preparing melon. Using a saw-tooth cut, remove top third of cantaloupe. Remove seeds. Loosen melon meat from rind. Slice meat into sections and serve with salad. Sprinkle inside of melon with lemon juice and fill hollow with salad. Trim with remaining egg. Serves four.

Crab-Grapefruit Salad

½ cup mayonnaise
2 tablespoons catsup
1 tablespoon lemon juice
Dash hot pepper sauce

Combine the above ingredients and chill while preparing:

1 cup crab meat
1 tablespoon lemon juice
1 one-pound can grapefruit sections
Lettuce leaves

Sprinkle crab meat with lemon juice and then alternate layers of crab and grapefruit sections in lettuce-lined sherbet glasses. Serve chilled with dressing poured over each serving. Serves six.

Crab and Rice Salad with Avocado

1 six-ounce package long-grain wild rice mix, prepared and cooled
1 cup crab meat or one seven and one-half ounce can crab meat
1 tablespoon lemon juice
2 tablespoons chopped canned pimiento
¼ cup chopped green pepper
2 tablespoons chopped fresh parsley
2 tablespoons Russian salad dressing
½ cup mayonnaise
2 medium avocados, peeled, pitted and sliced

Combine crab meat, lemon juice, cooled rice, green pepper, parsley and pimiento. Combine Russian dressing and mayonnaise and toss with crab mixture. Chill and serve with avocado slices. Serves four.

Crab-Artichoke Salad

2 cups crab meat
1 nine-ounce package frozen artichoke hearts, cooked, drained and chilled - or one 15-ounce can artichoke hearts, rinsed
and drained
2 hard boiled eggs, chopped
Salad greens
Salad dressing: recipe follows

In a salad bowl, toss salad greens and top with crab meat, ar-
tichokes and chopped eggs. Toss with following dressing just before
serving:

Salad Dressing

Whip one-half cup heavy cream and fold in one cup mayonnaise,
one-quarter cup chili sauce, two teaspoons lemon juice and salt to
taste. Chill. Serves four to six.

Crab Mold

1½ cups boiling water
2 three-ounce boxes lemon gelatin
1 cup chili sauce
1 cup mayonnaise
2 tablespoons sweet pickle relish
1 cup chopped celery
2 cups (or two seven and one-half ounce cans lump) crab meat
Sauce: recipe follows

In boiling water, dissolve gelatin and stir in chili sauce and mayonnaise. Chill until slightly thickened. Stir crab meat, relish and celery
into gelatin mixture. Turn into a six-cup mold and refrigerate overnight until firm.

Unmold and serve, garnished with black olives and cherry
tomatoes and this cucumber sauce:

Cucumber Sauce

Mix two cups sour cream and two cups of unpeeled, well-drained,
chopped cucumber, one tablespoon lemon juice and a pinch of sugar
and enough horseradish to give the sauce a slightly sharp taste.
Serves 10 to 12.

Simple Crab Salad

1 pound backfin lump crab meat
¾ cup chopped celery
½ teaspoon salt
2 tablespoons lemon juice
¼ cup mayonnaise
1 teaspoon capers

Combine celery, lemon juice, salt and pepper to taste, mayonnaise and capers. Add crab meat. Serve chilled. Serves four to six.

Crab-Pear Salad

2 cups crab meat
2 cups unpeeled, diced pears
¾ cup diced celery
½ cup mayonnaise
2 tablespoons lemon juice
½ teaspoon salt
Dash pepper
Lettuce leaves
Slivered, toasted almonds

Combine all ingredients, except lettuce leaves and almonds. Serve on lettuce leaves and garnish with toasted almonds. Serves four.

Crab Salad Deluxe with Vegetables

1 pound crab meat, lump
1 eight-ounce can green beans, drained
1 15-ounce can artichoke hearts, rinsed, drained and quartered
2 hard boiled eggs, chopped
½ cup chopped cucumber
½ cup sliced celery
¼ cup diced raw cauliflower or broccoli
¼ cup diced green pepper
Salt and pepper to taste
1 cup Thousand Island dressing
2 tomatoes, sliced
Lettuce leaves
Sliced radishes

Combine all ingredients, except lettuce, tomatoes and radishes. Divide into six portions and arrange on lettuce leaves, garnished with tomato slices and radishes. Serves six.

Crab-Spinach Salad

1 large avocado
1 tablespoon orange juice
1 pound fresh spinach, washed and torn in pieces
2 cups lump crab meat
3 oranges, sectioned
Salad dressing, recipe follows

Prepare salad dressing according to following directions. Chill. Just before serving, peel avocado and slice into rings. Sprinkle with orange juice. Combine spinach, avocado, crab and orange sections in a salad bowl and toss with this dressing:

⅔ cup salad oil
⅓ cup orange juice
2 tablespoons sugar
½ teaspoon grated rind of orange
1 tablespoon vinegar
¼ teaspoon salt
¼ teaspoon dry mustard
Dash hot pepper sauce

Combine all ingredients and shake well to mix. Makes one and a third-cups dressing.

Sandwiches

This recipe comes from the kitchen of one of the best cooks I know, Sara Parris, a good cook who has always been generous with advice and recipes.

Crab Meat on Holland Rusk

1 eight-ounce package cream cheese
1 seven and one-half ounce can crab meat
4 tablespoons mayonnaise
1 teaspoon grated onion
Juice of one lemon
½ teaspoon salt
Pepper to taste
Holland rusk
Tomato slices
Sliced cheese

Mix first seven ingredients well. Place on Holland Rusk and top each with one slice tomato and one slice cheese. Secure with toothpick and bake at 300 degrees until cheese melts. Serves five to six.

Broiled Crab Sandwich

1 cup crab meat
¼ cup chopped celery
½ cup unpeeled, chopped apple
1 tablespoon lemon juice
½ cup mayonnaise
3 hamburger buns, split
2 tablespoons butter or margarine, softened
6 slices sharp process American cheese

Blend first five ingredients. Spread butter on halves of buns and toast. Top each half with one-third cup of crab mixture. Broil four inches from heat for three to four minutes. Top each with a slice of cheese and broil until cheese begins to melt. Serves six.

Crab Boats

Crab salad, your own favorite recipe or one of preceding recipes (See "Simple Crab Salad")
6 hot dog buns
3 tablespoons butter or margarine, softened

Open buns slightly and spread with softened butter. Grill for two or three minutes to toast. Fill buns with chilled crab salad. Serves six.

Hot Open-face Crab Sandwich

1 cup or one seven and one-half ounce can crab meat
¼ cup mayonnaise
1 egg yolk
1 three-ounce package cream cheese, softened
¼ teaspoon prepared mustard
1 teaspoon minced onion
3 English muffins, split and toasted
2 tablespoons butter or margarine, softened

Combine crab meat and mayonnaise and set aside. Beat together the cream cheese, egg yolk, mustard and onion. Spread toasted muffin halves with butter, then crab mixture and finally with cream cheese mixture. On a baking sheet, broil sandwiches five to six inches from heat until golden and bubbly, about two or three minutes. Serves six.

Crab Party Sandwich

1 cup crab meat or one seven and one-half ounce can crab meat
2 tablespoons lemon juice
2 tablespoons mayonnaise
1 medium avocado, peeled, pitted and mashed
1 tablespoon minced green onion
Dash freshly ground pepper
3 English muffins, split and toasted
Mayonnaise
Lettuce
3 hard boiled eggs, sliced
1 two-ounce jar caviar

Combine crab meat, lemon juice, mayonnaise, avocado, onion and pepper. Chill.

Spread muffin halves with some mayonnaise and top each with a lettuce leaf. Arrange egg slices over lettuce and spoon crab mixture over egg. Top each with a rounded teaspoon of caviar. Serves six.

This hearty sandwich comes from the files of Shirley Lee. She says it hails from New York, but other than that, neither of us is sure of its origins. I have a hunch about it though, and that is that this conglomeration is named after that comic-strip character who is famous for his sandwich creations.

Bumsteads

1 cup crab meat or one seven and one-half ounce can crab meat
¼ cup chopped pickle, sweet or dill
1 tablespoon minced onion
3 eggs, hard-boiled and chopped
¼ cup American cheese, diced
2 tablespoons mayonnaise
8 hotdog rolls, buttered

Combine first six ingredients and divide between the hotdog rolls. Wrap separately in aluminum foil and bake at 350 degrees for about 15 minutes or until heated through.

Soups and Stews

Cream of Crab

1 pound crab meat
1 cup boiling water
1 vegetable bouillon cube
1 small onion, chopped, about one-half cup
¼ cup margarine or butter, melted
2 tablespoon all-purpose flour
1 teaspoon salt
Dash freshly ground black pepper
4 drops hot pepper sauce
1 quart high-fat milk or half-and-half

Dissolve bouillon in boiling water. Saute' onion in margarine, until transparent. Blend in flour and cook stirring, until thickened. Add hot pepper sauce, salt and peppers. Slowly stir in bouillon and milk or cream. Stir and cook over medium heat until slightly thickened. Stir in crab meat and heat through. Serve garnished with parsley, if desired and adjust seasoning. Serves six.

Crab-Asparagus Soup

1 quart chicken broth
1 14-ounce can cut asparagus
1 seven and one-half ounce can crab meat or one cup fresh crab meat
3 egg yolks, beaten
2 tablespoons soy sauce
3 tablespoons cornstarch
¼ cup water

Heat chicken broth and add a small amount to beaten yolks. Slowly stir egg yolks into broth. Add drained asparagus and soy sauce. Combine the cornstarch and water to make a smooth paste. Add to soup, stirring constantly until smooth and slightly thickened. Stir crab meat into soup and heat to a boil. Simmer five minutes. Serves six.

Quick Crab Bisque

1 10½-ounce can cream of mushroom soup
1 10½-ounce cream of asparagus soup
2 cups milk
1 cup half-and-half
1 cup crab meat
¼ cup dry sherry

Combine all ingredients, except for sherry. Heat to boiling. Stir in sherry and serve. Serves six.

Real "She-crab Soup" is only made from the female crab, the Sook. The distinction here is that the eggs are added to the soup. This traditional soup is a specialty of Charleston, S.C., where crabs are plentiful. Reportedly the "she-crabs" always brought higher prices than the "he-crabs" there. During colonial times George Washington visited Charleston and was so impressed with the celebrated soup, that after his visit there in 1791, he spread the word of this special delicacy all the way to New England.

With possession of egg-bearing female crabs, "spongers," illegal in most areas, those who want to taste this regional dish may have to resort to the recipe option of placing crumbled hard-boiled egg yolks in the bottoms of their soup bowls. As with most regional specialties, there is usually more than one version. Here are three, plus a "Crab and Lobster Soup."

She-crab Soup I

1 pound lump crab meat and roe or eggs
6 tablespoons butter
1 tablespoon all-purpose flour
2 cups light cream or half-and-half
1 cup milk
1 teaspoon Worcestershire sauce
1 teaspoon each salt and grated lemon peel
¼ teaspoon each ground mace and white pepper
3 soda crackers, crumbled
4 tablespoons dry sherry
½ cup whipping cream, whipped
Paprika

Melt butter and blend in flour in the top of double boiler. Add half-and-half and milk and, stirring, add Worcestershire, salt, lemon peel, mace, crab meat and eggs. Cook slowly for 20 minutes. Season to taste with salt and pepper and add cracker crumbs. Set aside and allow to stand in a warm place for 10 to 15 minutes. Serve in heated soup bowls, adding a teaspoon of sherry to each bowl. Top with a dollop of whipped cream and dust with paprika. Serves six to eight.

She-crab Soup II

4 tablespoons butter
¼ cup onion, minced
2 cups milk
½ teaspoon lemon rind
2 cups heavy cream
¼ cup cracker crumbs
1 pound lump crab meat
Salt, pepper, nutmeg and cayenne pepper to taste
1 tablespoon dry sherry
½ cup crab roe or crab eggs, if available

In a heavy saucepan or top of a double boiler, melt butter and add onion to saute'. Stir in milk and lemon rind and simmer for five minutes.

Add cream and crab meat and heat slowly, simmering over boiling water for 15 minutes, stirring occasionally. Stir in cracker crumbs and seasonings to taste. Before serving, stir in sherry and crab roe and heat through. Serves six.

She-crab Soup III

1 tablespoon butter
1 quart high-fat milk
Few drops onion juice
¼ teaspoon ground mace
½ teaspoon Worcestershire sauce
Pepper to taste
1 teaspoon flour
2 cups white lump crab meat and crab eggs or roe
4 tablespoons dry sherry
¼ pint heavy cream, whipped

Melt the butter in the top of a double boiler and blend in flour until smooth and slightly thickened. Add milk, gradually, stirring constantly. Add crab meat, eggs and all seasonings, except for sherry.

Place one tablespoon sherry in each of four warmed soup bowls and add soup. Top with whipped cream. Sprinkle with paprika or chopped parsley. If unable to obtain "she-crabs" with eggs, sprinkle crumbled hard boiled eggs yolk in bottom of soup bowls. Serves four.

Crab-Lobster Soup

4 cups Italian plum tomatoes, cooked until reduced to a paste
1 cup fresh green peas, cooked and sieved
1 cup milk
2 cups heavy cream
1 pound lump crab meat
1 one and a half-pound lobster, cooked
Salt and freshly ground black pepper to taste
1 tablespoon Worcestershire
¼ teaspoon ground ginger
Cayenne pepper to taste
½ cup dry sherry
6 tablespoons dry sherry
6 tablespoons whipped cream
Paprika and chopped fresh parsley

Combine paste made of tomatoes and sieved or mashed peas and add milk, cream and crab meat. Remove meat from lobster cut in bite-size pieces and add to crab mixture. Add salt, peppers, ginger and Worcestershire sauce. Simmer one hour, stirring frequently.

Add half of sherry. To serve, add one tablespoon sherry to each of six heated soup bowls. Ladle in soup and garnish each with one tablespoon whipped cream and dust with paprika.

Cream of Crab Soup -- South Carolina-Style

1 tablespoon butter or margarine, melted
1 medium onion, chopped
1 quart chicken stock
1 quart light cream or half-and-half
½ teaspoon each ground mace and celery salt
2 tablespoons chopped parsley
Freshly ground pepper and salt to taste
1 pound crab meat, lump preferably
2 tablespoons all-purpose flour
¼ cup dry sherry

In a large stock pot, saute' onion in melted butter until transparent. Add chicken stock and cream. Stir in seasonings and crab meat. Simmer 10 to 15 minutes. Meanwhile, make a paste with the flour and a little water. Stirring, stir paste into soup to thicken it. Remove from heat and add sherry just before serving. Serves eight.

Crab Gumbo

12 large crabs, cleaned and quartered, but not cooked
1 cup butter or margarine
3 cups chopped onion
2 tablespoons flour
3 quarts water
1 cup ham, chopped (preferably country ham)
Salt and pepper to taste
2 tablespoons file' powder
Hot rice

Prepare crabs and set aside. Melt butter in stock pot and saute' onion until tender. Stir in flour and cook over med-low heat until slightly browned. To this roux, or mixture, add the crabs, water and ham. Season to taste and cover. Simmer one to one and a half hours. Just before serving, stir in file' powder. Do not boil. Ladle over hot rice. Serves 10 to 12.

Like the previous recipe for crab gumbo, gumbos are a specialty of Louisiana and are more stews than soups. The file' powder, used to thicken some gumbos,is made from sassafras leaves. That southern vegetable, okra, is often an ingredient in gumbo, as it is in the following recipe. The name "gumbo" was derived from the African word for okra and the okra is used to thicken the stew.

Seafood-Okra Gumbo

¼ cup vegetable oil
3 pounds fresh okra, thinly sliced
⅓ cup each all-purpose flour and vegetable oil, mixed
3 cups chopped onion
1 quart water
2 tablespoons tomato paste
2 pounds shrimp, peeled and deveined
1 pound crab meat
1 cup ham, diced
1 pint oysters
½ cup freshly-chopped parsley (four tablespoons if dried)
2 cloves garlic, chopped
3 bay leaves
1 cup celery, chopped
Hot pepper sauce to taste
Hot cooked rice

In the one-quarter cup oil, saute' the okra until thick. Set aside. In a heavy stock pot, cook and stir the paste made of the oil and flour until it is thick and browned, about 20 minutes. Add onion, water and tomato paste. Stir in the okra, then the shrimp, crab, ham and oysters. Stir in the parsley, garlic, bay leaves and celery. Simmer, uncovered, about one hour. Season to taste with pepper and salt and the hot pepper sauce.

Serve over hot rice. Serves 12.

Another Creole dish is jambalaya. Traditionally jambalaya is a rice dish cooked with tomatoes seafood, meat or poultry and onions and herbs. The dish was believed to have been introduced into the cookery of Louisiana when the Spanish controlled New Orleans. Jambalaya resembles that traditional Spanish dish, paella. Jambalaya is eaten as a stew and served in a bowl.

Crab Jambalaya

6 slices bacon, chopped and fried crispy
1 medium onion, chopped
½ cup celery, chopped
¼ cup green pepper, chopped
¼ cup uncooked long-grain rice, not instant
1 can (28 ounces) tomatoes, cut up

Salt and pepper to taste
1 cup crab meat or one seven and one-half ounce can crab
meat
1 teaspoon Worcestershire sauce

Reserve two tablespoons drippings from bacon and in it saute' the
onion, celery and green pepper. Add tomatoes with juice from can
and rice. Simmer until the rice is tender, about 20-25 minutes, stirring occasionally. Stir in Worcestershire sauce and crab meat. Heat
through and serve in bowls, topping with reserved bacon. Serves
four to six.

This following recipe evolved from my favorite method for preparing conch chowder. It first contained only conch. I sometimes use
minced clams and the one day when we had some cooked crab claws
from a crab feast from the previous evening, my husband suggested
adding the claw meat to the chowder. The result was delicious and
this has become a tradition at our house. Fresh or canned crab may
be used, but that special feeling of accomplishment that comes from
securing one's own food "for free" may be missing if the canned crab
is used.

Crab-Clam Chowder

3 carrots, scraped and thinly sliced
1 green pepper, chopped
1 large onion, chopped
1 rib celery, thinly sliced
2 tablespoons salad oil
1 28-ounce can tomatoes, cut up, juice reserved
2 cups water (add more if necessary)
2 tablespoons catsup or chili sauce
2 drops hot pepper sauce or more to taste
½ teaspoon dried basil
¼ teaspoon freshly-ground pepper
1 tablespoon Worcestershire sauce
1 tablespoon minced parsley
3 potatoes, scrubbed and cubed, but unpeeled
1 cup crab claw meat or one 7½-ounce can crab meat
1 six and one-half ounce can minced clams, juice reserved

In a three quart or larger sauce pan, saute' the carrots, green pepper, onion and celery in the salad oil, until they soften slightly. Add
the remaining ingredients and stir to combine. Bring to a boil, then

reduce heat, cover and simmer about 30 minutes, or until vegetables are tender. Adjust seasonings. Serves six.

Main Dishes

Deviled Crab en Casserole

1½ cups each soft bread crumbs and milk
2 cups crab meat
5 hard boiled eggs
½ cup butter, melted
½ teaspoon dry mustard
1/8 teaspoon red pepper
Fine dry bread crumbs
White wine -- about four tablespoons

Combine soft bread crumbs and milk and stir in crab meat and the whites (chopped) of the hard boiled eggs. Season to taste and stir in melted butter and three to four tablespoons white wine. Mash the egg yolks and stir in. Turn into a buttered casserole and cover top with dry bread crumbs and dot with butter.

Bake at 350 degrees for 30 minutes. Serves six.

Manicotti with Crab Sauce

1 cup chopped onion
1 clove garlic, minced
2 tablespoons vegetable oil
1 one-pound can tomatoes, chopped
1 eight-ounce can tomato sauce
1 teaspoon basil
1 cup crab meat or one seven and one-half ounce can crab meat
8 manicotti shells
1 cup Parmesan cheese, grated and divided
2 beaten eggs
2 cups large curd cottage cheese
2 tablespoons chopped parsley

Prepare the sauce by cooking onion and garlic in the oil. Add tomatoes, tomato sauce, basil and simmer 25-30 minutes. Stir in crab meat and spread one third of sauce on bottom of shallow one and a half-quart baking dish.

Prepare manicotti shells according to package directions, drain and rinse. Beat together one half-cup of the Parmesan cheese, eggs, cottage cheese and parsley. Fill shells with this cheese mixture and arrange on top of sauce in casserole. Spoon remaining sauce over filled shells and bake, covered, for 25 minutes or until shells are hot and filling is set. Sprinkle with remaining cheese before serving. Serves four.

Crab-Fish Casserole

1 one-pound package frozen fish fillets (not breaded) thawed and drained
½ cup butter or margarine, melted
1 cup herb-seasoned stuffing mix, crushed
1 cup crab meat or one seven and one-half ounce can or one six-ounce package frozen crab meat, thawed
1 four-ounce can mushrooms, drained
1 egg
2 tablespoons chopped parsley
¼ teaspoon salt
2 tablespoons lemon juice
Topping of one-half cup crushed herb seasoned stuffing mix, mixed with two tablespoons melted butter or margarine

Arrange fish fillets in bottom of eight-inch square ungreased baking dish. Combine the one-half cup melted butter, the one cup stuffing mix, the crab meat, mushrooms, egg, parsley, salt and lemon juice. Sprinkle over fish fillets and then sprinkle topping over crab mixture. Bake at 350 degrees for 30 to 35 minutes or until heated through and fish flakes with a fork. Serves four.

Flounder Stuffed With Crab

1 cup minced onion
½ cup minced celery
½ cup chopped fresh parsley
¼ cup minced green pepper
2 cloves garlic, minced
½ cup butter or margarine, melted
1 tablespoon all-purpose flour
½ cup each white wine and milk

2 cups crab meat
1 cup seasoned dry breadcrumbs
Salt and pepper to taste
6 flounder fillets (10-ounces each)
Mornay Sauce, recipe follows

Saute' onion, celery, parsley, green pepper and garlic in butter until tender. Add flour and cook another minute, stirring. Gradually add milk and wine and cook until thickened slightly, stirring constantly. Remove from heat and stir in crab meat, bread crumbs and salt and pepper. Arrange three of the fillets on a jellyroll pan and spoon about one cup crab mixture on each. Cut remaining fillets in half lengthwise and place a fillet half on either side of each of the stuffed fillets, pressing gently into stuffing mixture. Spoon mornay sauce on top of each and sprinkle with paprika.

Bake at 425 degrees for 15 to 20 minutes or until fish flakes easily. If desired, spoon or pipe hot mashed potatoes around each portion. Garnish with aditional paprika and parsley. Cut each fillet in half to serve. Serves six.

Mornay Sauce

¼ cup butter
¼ cup all-purpose flour
2 cups milk
Salt and white pepper to taste
2 egg yolks, beaten until thick and lemon colored
2 tablespoons heavy cream
¼ cup shredded Swiss cheese

Melt butter and add flour and cook one minute. Gradually add milk, stirring constantly to avoid lumping, and cook until thickened and bubbly. Stir in salt and pepper. Add a small amount of milk mixture to beaten egg yolks and then add to the remaining milk mixture. Stirring constantly, cook until thickened, about two minutes. Add cheese and stir until melted. Makes two cups.

Crab Mornay

1 cup grated cheese
1 cup crab meat or one seven and one-half ounce can crab meat
2 tablespoons butter
2 tablespoons flour
1½ cups milk
Salt and pepper

Make a white sauce by melting butter and adding flour. Stir and cook about one minute. Gradually add milk and cook and stir until thickened. Add the crab meat and grated cheese. Season with salt and pepper and turn into a buttered casserole. Bake at 375 degrees until top is browned. Serves two.

Louisiana Crab

½ cup chopped onion
2 tablespoons butter
1 tablespoon all purpose flour
4 medium size tomatoes, peeled and coarsley chopped
1 cup water
¼ cup chopped green pepper
1 tablespoon chopped fresh parsley
2 teaspoons Worcestershire sauce
1 cup crab meat or one seven and one-half ounce can crab meat
Salt and pepper to taste

Saute' onion in butter. Add flour and let it brown slightly. Add tomatoes, water, green pepper and parsley. Season with Worcestershire, salt and pepper. Add crab meat and simmer 15 to 20 minutes. Serves four.

Crab Cakes, Eastern-Shore Style

1 pound fresh crab meat
1 egg beaten
1 hard cooked egg, chopped
Salt and pepper to taste
½ cup melted butter
1 tablespoon lemon juice
1 tablespoon Worcestershire sauce
Soft bread crumbs
Butter for frying

Combine crab meat, eggs, salt and pepper, butter, lemon juice and Worcestershire sauce. Add just enough bread crumbs to hold shape. Shape into small cakes.

Fry crab cakes slowly on each side in butter until browned. Serves eight.

Deluxe Deviled Crab

1 pound crab meat
1½ cups cracker crumbs, divided
½ cup finely chopped onion
¼ cup chopped parsley
1 teaspoon dry mustard
1 tablespoon lemon juice
1 teaspoon Worcestershire sauce
Dash each of hot pepper sauce and cayenne pepper
⅔ cup melted butter or margarine
¼ cup undiluted evaporated milk or heavy cream
Salt and pepper to taste
Butter

Combine crab meat and one cup of the crumbs and the rest of the ingredients, except for the additional butter. Spoon into six individual casseroles or cleaned crab shells. Sprinkle with the remaining crumbs and dot with butter. Bake at 375 degrees for 10 to 20 minutes or until browned on top. Serves six.

Crab Meat With Macaroni

3 tablespoons all-purpose flour
2 tablespoons butter or margarine
½ pound fresh mushrooms
1 cup milk
½ cup heavy cream
1 egg yolk, beaten
4 capers, chopped
½ teaspoon salt
1 pound fresh crab meat
Dash paprika
4 cups cooked macaroni
¼ cup white wine

Brown flour in the butter and saute' mushrooms in another pan. Gradually add the liquid from the sauteed mushrooms to the flour mixture, stirring to make a smooth paste. Gradually add the milk, stirring and cooking until thick and smooth. Add cream, mushrooms, capers, salt and paprika. Simmer 10 minutes, stirring occasionally. Add a small amount of this hot liquid to the egg yolk and then stir egg yolk mixture into milk mixture. Add crab meat and macaroni and heat through. Remove from heat and stir in wine. Serves eight.

Crab Cakes Walther

2 cups fresh crab meat
½ cup chopped onion
¼ cup finely chopped green pepper
2 slices stale whole wheat bread whirled in blender to make crumbs
1 tablespoon salad oil
2 tablespoons mayonnaise
2 eggs, beaten
½ teaspoon Worcestershire sauce
Salt and cayenne pepper to taste
Butter or margarine for frying

Combine salad oil and bread crumbs and, set aside while preparing onions and peppers. Add beaten eggs to bread mixture, then onion and peppers, Worcestershire sauce, mayonnaise, salt and pepper. Add crab meat, mixing lightly, but thoroughly. On a well-buttered griddle drop one-quarter cupful of this mixture and flatten slightly with spatula. Saute' over med-low heat four or five minutes on each side, or until delicately browned. Serves four. (Leftovers can be reheated or served on buns for tasty sandwiches.)

Baked Crab and Shrimp I

1 cup diced celery
¼ cup chopped green pepper
1 cup shelled, cooked shrimp, halved lengthwise
1 cup crab meat or one seven and one-half ounce can crab meat
¼ cup minced onion
1 teaspoon Worcestershire sauce
¾ cup mayonnaise
1 cup soft bread crumbs
1 tablespoon melted butter or margarine

Combine celery, green pepper, shrimp, crab, onion, Worcestershire sauce and mayonnaise. Turn into a buttered one-quart casserole dish. Toss bread crumbs with melted butter and sprinkle over top of casserole. Bake at 350 degrees, about 30 to 35 minutes, or until heated through. Serves four.

Baked Crab and Shrimp II

2 tablespoons grated Parmesan cheese
1 can (10½-ounces) cream of celery soup
¼ cup milk
1 egg, slightly beaten
1 cup crab meat or one seven and one-half ounce can crab meat
½ cup shrimp, cooked, shelled and deveined or
  one can (4½ ounces) shrimp, drained
1 can (3 ounces) mushrooms, drained
¼ cup dry bread crumbs
2 tablespoons Parmesan cheese
1 tablespoon melted butter or margarine

Combine first four ingredients in a small saucepan and heat over low heat until cheese is melted and mixture is heated. Stir in crab meat, shrimp and mushrooms and spoon into four individual casseroles or large shells. Combine bread crumbs, the two tablespoons Parmesan cheese and melted butter and sprinkle this mixture over the four casseroles.

Bake at 375 degrees for 20 minutes. Serves four.

Crab Newburg

This following recipe is rich due to the addition of heavy cream. Legend has it that the recipe was named for a rather modest bon vivant by the name of Wenburg who scrambled his name to escape notoriety when naming this famous dish.

Crab Newburg

1 pound fresh crab meat
2 tablespoons butter, melted
3 tablespoons dry sherry
1 cup heavy cream
2 egg yolks, beaten
Salt, cayenne pepper to taste

Saute' the crab meat in the butter, but do not let it brown. Season with salt and cayenne and stir in sherry. Cook one minute, then add cream. When the mixture comes to a boil, stir a small amount of it into the egg yolks. When they are heated, add this to the crab mixture.

Do not allow to boil, but heat until thickened slightly. Serve on toast points. Serves four to six.

Stuffed Crab Shells

1 pound crab meat
1 small onion, diced
½ cup diced green pepper
2 eggs, beaten slightly
36 saltine crackers, pulverized
¼ cup mayonnaise
2 tablespoons prepared mustard
1 teaspoon steak sauce
Milk to moisten
Salt and pepper to taste

Combine all ingredients in order given and divide between eight buttered crab shells. Bake at 300 degrees for 35 minutes or until heated through, and golden. Serves eight.

Western Deviled Crab

3 scallions chopped, including tops
1 clove garlic, minced
6 fresh mushrooms, sliced
1 green pepper, diced
5 tablespoons butter, divided
⅔ cup dry white wine
1 tablespoon dry mustard
3 tablespoons all-purpose flour
2 cups half-and-half, milk and cream
Salt, cayenne and freshly ground black pepper to taste
1 tablespoon prepared chutney
1½ pounds crab meat
½ cup buttered soft bread crumbs
2 tablespoons grated Parmesan cheese

Saute' the scallions, garlic, mushrooms and pepper in two tablespoons of the butter. Add wine and dry mustard and cook to reduce the liquid by one-third.

In a saucepan, melt the remaining butter and stir in flour, cream and season with salt and peppers. Bring to a boil, stirring to keep smooth. Then cover and cook 10 minutes.

Stir vegetable mixture into this sauce. Add the chutney and crab meat. Turn into buttered individual casseroles or large buttered baking dish. Combine bread crumbs and cheese and sprinkle this over casseroles.

Bake at 400 degrees 10 minutes for the individual casseroles, about 25 minutes for one large one. Serves six.

Crab Quiche

1 unbaked nine-inch pie shell
1½ cups crab meat
2 green onions, sliced, including tops
1 cup shredded Swiss cheese
3 eggs, beaten
1 cup light cream
¼ teaspoon dry mustard
Dash nutmeg
¼ cup sliced almonds

Scatter crab meat over bottom of pie shell and top with sliced onions and shredded cheese. In a small bowl beat together the eggs, cream, mustard and nutmeg just to combine evenly. Pour over crab and cheese and top with almonds. Bake at 325 degrees about 45 minutes, or until set. Remove from oven and let stand about 10 minutes before cutting. Serves six.

Crab Crepes

(Crepes recipe follows)

½ cup chicken broth
1 cup light cream
3 tablespoons all-purpose flour
Salt and pepper to taste
2 tablespoons grated Parmesan cheese
2 tablespoons dry sherry
1 cup crab meat
½ cup sliced water chestnuts
2 tablespoons sliced pimientos
1 one-pound asparagus spears, drained
Parmesan cheese

Prepare crepes browning only on one side. Set crepes aside.

Combine chicken broth, cream and flour in a saucepan. Heat to boiling, stirring until smooth and thickened. Season with salt and pepper and stir in two tablespoons Parmesan cheese, dry sherry, water chestnuts, crab meat and pimientos. Heat through.

Place one stalk of asparagus on a crepe. Spread with one and one-half tablespoons of crab sauce and roll. Place in a buttered casserole, preparing remaining asparagus and crepes in this manner. Sprinkle with additional Parmesan cheese and bake at 300 degrees about 30 minutes, or until heated through. Serve with remaining crab sauce. Serves four to six.

Crepes

1 cup all-purpose flour
Dash salt
3 eggs
2 tablespoons melted butter
1¼ cups milk

Beat ingredients until blended, but do not overbeat or crepes will be tough.

Let batter stand at least one hour before baking. Ingredients may be mixed in blender or food processor. Can be prepared the night before and refrigerated overnight before baking.

Brush crepe pan with melted butter and using a hot pan, pour in two to three tablespoons crepe batter and quickly tilt pan to spread batter to cover bottom of pan. Cook one to two minutes, or until bottom is lightly browned and blistered. If cooking both sides, the second side will cook in about 30 seconds. Stack crepes with a piece of waxed paper between to keep them from sticking while preparing the rest of the batter. Left-over crepes can be wrapped and frozen for later use. Unfilled crepes can be wrapped and refrigerated up to four days or frozen up to two months.

Plantation-style Sautéed Crab

8 slices thick bacon, diced and fried crisp
¼ cup each chopped green pepper and green onion
1 pound fresh crab meat
2 tablespoons butter
1 teaspoon Worcestershire sauce
Salt and white pepper to taste
¼ cup dry white wine
1 cup hot chicken stock
2 eggs, beaten
¼ cup cracker crumbs
¼ cup grated Parmesan cheese, divided

Fry bacon and reserve two tablespoons drippings. Saute the green pepper and onion in bacon drippings. Add butter and crab meat to pan and cook one minute. Stir in Worcestershire sauce, pepper, wine, chicken stock and eggs in order given. Stir in cracker crumbs and one half of the quarter cup of grated cheese. Turn into a casserole and top with remaining cheese. Broil three to five minutes or until top is evenly browned. Serve with lemon wedges if desired. Serves four to six.

Fried Soft-Shelled Crabs I

Cleaned soft-shelled crabs (see illustrations)
Corn meal or flour
Butter
Salt and pepper to taste

Roll each cleaned crab in flour or cornmeal. Melt enough butter to cover the bottom of a small frying pan. Saute' the crab slowly on each side, about three to five minutes on each side, until crispy and golden and cooked through, but not dried out. Season with salt and pepper and serve with buttered toast if desired.

If preparing several soft-shell crabs in this manner, chopped fresh parsley and about one half cup chopped scallions can be added to the butter in the pan when frying the crabs. But since the strong flavor of onions and parsley may detract from the delicate flavors of the soft shelled crabs, some prefer to let their soft shells cook solo.

Fried Soft-Shelled Crabs II

Cleaned soft-shelled crabs, count on three or four per person
2 cups flour
1 cup milk
1 large egg
Deep fat for frying
Salt and pepper to taste

Make a smooth batter by beating the flour, milk and egg together. Drain cleaned crabs and dip in this batter. Fry in deep hot fat at about 350 degrees about five minutes, or until crabs are golden brown. Drain on absorbent paper.

Rounding out the recipes is this traditional fare from the Deep South. Like the famous Northern tradition of a clam bake, the Southern seafood boil provides a full meal, all cooked in one big pot and all redolent of the seafood it contains. In the coastal areas of the South, a seafood boil is one of the favorite get-togethers. Like many dishes of this type, the dimensions are changeable to fit the diners. Count heads and double expectations when preparing a seafood boil.

Southern Seafood Boil

½ cup salt
20 small onions, peeled
12 potatoes, scrubbed, unpeeled
3 garlic bulbs
1 three-ounce package crab boil
1 cup vinegar
5 lemons, halved
3 dozen crabs
12 ears corn, halved
6 pounds shrimp, unpeeled

Fill a six gallon pot two-thirds full with water and add salt. Bring to a boil and add potatoes and onions; cover and cook over high heat 20 minutes. Stir in crab boil, crabs, garlic, vinegar and lemons. Reduce heat and simmer 10 minutes. Add corn and simmer five minutes and remove pot from heat. Add shrimp and let stand five minutes, covered. Drain water and arrange seafoods and vegetables on a platter. Serve with melted butter and cocktail sauce. Serves eight to 12.

Glossary

Apron . . . Abdominal covering shell of the crab. Female crabs carry eggs under apron, which becomes distended as eggs mature.

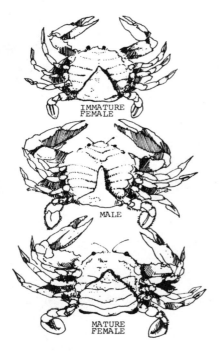

Atlantic blue crab . . . Callinectes sapidus

Backfin . . . Solid chunk of white crab meat located at base of swimming fin, also called jumbo lump.

Buck and rider . . . Doublers or male and female Atlantic blue crabs in cradle-carrying position

Buckram . . . Soft-shelled crab, one day after it has shed its shell

Buster . . . Atlantic blue crab that is ready to shed its shell and become a soft-shell crab

Callinectes sapidus . . . Atlantic blue crab

Carapace . . . Shell or hard covering of Atlantic blue crab

Chicken necker . . . A regional term (sometimes derogatory) denoting someone who fishes for crabs using chicken necks for bait, also used to describe non-resident weekend crabbers

Cradle carrying . . . Position in which male crab carries soft-shelled female crab for purpose of impregnating her and also to protect the female until her shell hardens. Lasts two to three days. These pairs of crabs are also called doublers.

Crustacea . . . Class of invertebrates to which the Atlantic blue crab belongs

Dead man's fingers . . . Elongated spongy-looking organs, gills. Remove when cleaning crabs.

Doublers . . . See cradle carrying

Ecdysis . . . The act of shedding the old shell when it is outgrown. Will result in a crab about one-third larger in size, with a soft shell which takes two to three days to harden.

Flake . . . Classification of crab meat, white meat other than backfin. Comes from anterior chambers of crab.

Green crab . . . One of stages of crabs prior to becoming soft-shell crab (i.e. very green, green to ripe)

Jimmy . . . Male Atlantic blue crab, distinguishable by T-shaped apron.

Jimmy potting . . . Use of a male crab as bait to lure third-season un-impregnated female crabs into crab pot. These female crabs become soft-shelled crabs soon after they are caught in this manner. Done in spring.

Length . . . Actually the width of crab across top of its shell between the outermost points. A five-inch length is legal limit in most areas.

Molting . . . See Ecdysis

Paper shells . . . Soft-shelled crab about 12 hours after it sheds its shell. Shell is slightly stiff.

Peeler . . . Atlantic blue crab which is shedding its shell

Portunids . . . Members of the swimming crab family to which Atlantic blue crabs belong

Rank . . . "Red sign" crabs, ready to shed shells

Sally . . . Sexually immature female crab, also called a Snot. Has triangular-shaped apron.

Scapping . . . Method of catching crabs on foot in the water using a long-handled dip net to scoop them up

She crab . . . Female crab

Shedding . . . See Ecdysis

Slabs . . . Especially large crabs, also called "Whales"

Snot . . . Sexually immature female Atlantic blue crabs. See Sally.

Soft-shell crab . . . Atlantic blue crab which has shed its hard shell. A delicacy in which the shell is eaten along with the crab

Sook . . . Sexually mature female Atlantic blue crab. Has bell-shaped abdominal apron.

Sponger . . . Female Atlantic blue crab which is carrying eggs under abdominal apron. Illegal to catch or possess in most areas

Whale . . . Especially large Atlantic blue crab. See Slabs

BLUE CRAB

HOW TO MEASURE   INCHES

Index